Evaluating
School Busing

James E. Teele

The Praeger Special Studies program—utilizing the most modern and efficient book production techniques and a selective worldwide distribution network—makes available to the academic, government, and business communities significant, timely research in U.S. and international economic, social, and political development.

Evaluating School Busing

Case Study of Boston's Operation Exodus

PRAEGER SPECIAL STUDIES IN U.S. ECONOMIC, SOCIAL, AND POLITICAL ISSUES

Praeger Publishers   New York   Washington   London

Library of Congress Cataloging in Publication Data

Teele, James E
    Evaluating school busing.

    (Praeger special studies in U.S. economic,
social, and political issues)
    1. School children—Transportation—Boston—
Case studies.   2. School integration—Boston—Case
studies.   I. Title.   II. Title: Case study of Boston's
operation Exodus.
LA306. B7T43   372. 1'8'7   72-12465

PRAEGER PUBLISHERS
111 Fourth Avenue, New York, N.Y. 10003, U.S.A.
5, Cromwell Place, London SW7 2JL, England

Published in the United States of America in 1973
by Praeger Publishers, Inc.

Printed in the United States of America

For Bessie, Joseph, and Ann

PREFACE

Early one morning, September 8, 1965, Operation Exodus unfolded. Poor black parents, with much community support, initiated a school busing program whereby several hundred black children of all ages between 5 and 14 were to be bused from nearly all-black schools in the black community to predominantly or all-white schools in surrounding communities within the limits of the city of Boston. This was, so far as I know, the first such undertaking initiated by blacks in any community in the United States. Indeed, it was analogous to the first shot in a war.

Although the parties to the conflict presented many and shifting rationales, there never seemed to be any real communication between the chief opponents: the Boston School Committee and the black parents whose children were involved. The present book is part of the story of the conflict as I saw it. It is also a report of my attempt to evaluate the effects of the busing of black children.

With one exception this report is written largely as I experienced it, i.e., the chapters and the material presented in them follow approximately the chronological order of my experience. The exception is Chapter 1, where some educational experiences of Boston blacks in the period 1845-55 are discussed. I think the reader's awareness of this historical background will better enable him to appreciate the problems encountered during the attempt at evaluation. My research was well under way when I became aware of this material. The conclusions arrived at were reached at the "end" of the study.

In Chapter 2 I present my early experience with the group of parents (Operation Exodus) who are the subject of this book. These parents, black parents, undertook an effort to improve the quality of their children's education in the public schools of Boston. Early descriptive findings for this period (phase 1) based on interviews with the parents are presented in the chapter; in addition the limitations of the phase 1 research are presented.

In Chapter 3 I present the research design for phase 2; this phase of the research plan describes the data to be collected on the children of the parents described in Chapter 2. While the phase 2 plan was designed to collect data on the children and their parents, it is emphasized that the main thrust of phase 2 research was to be directed at the children.

In Chapters 4 and 5 various problems encountered during the research implementation of phase 2 are presented. The ways in which these problems were met are discussed; inevitably it became necessary to alter the research plan—and this had serious consequences for the evaluation effort. These chapters could be of great value for those involved in evaluation, especially when the program under evaluation or the evaluation of a program could have political and policy ramifications (as when the evaluative results point or could point to a reordering of statuses, a redistribution of resources, or a sharing of decision-making powers).

Some findings with regard to the children and parents are presented in Chapters 6 and 7. Although the original design was altered, it seemed appropriate to make a serious attempt to salvage the research on the children. This attempt was made, with results the reader can judge. The chapter on the parents (Chapter 7) describes the growth and some of the achievements of the organization. In addition case vignettes, intended to underscore individual achievements by some of the parents, are presented.

Implications of my attempted evaluation for both (a) other researchers contemplating the evaluation of politically sensitive programs and (b) the formation of educational programs and policies with regard to blacks are presented in the concluding Chapter 8.

It is hoped that the report that follows will attract—not repel— sociologists and other social scientists to the challenge of evaluative research in politically sensitive areas.

It is, of course, difficult to recall and to cite the names of all the persons and organizations that have participated in the research study reported on here. Still, there are some that deserve special mention.

I am most grateful to all of the parents and children in Operation Exodus who participated in this study as subjects; I am also grateful to those parents in Exodus who lent their encouragement and research assistance to the conduct of the study. In particular, Ellen Jackson, Audrey Butler, Marlene M. McIlvaine, Jeanette Bowen, Barbara Pitts, Mary Davis, and Ralph Trotman gave invaluable assistance to me.

A number of my colleagues were important to the study because they encouraged me to undertake it. Bernie Kramer of the University of Massachusetts (Boston) and William M. Schmidt of the Harvard School of Public Health were most instrumental in encouraging the undertaking of the research. Moreover, William Schmidt, head of the Department of Maternal and Child Health at Harvard, the department in which I was employed when the study was undertaken, never questioned my initiating the early stage of this project in 1965 without any outside research support. Other colleagues have assisted me greatly by reading all or parts of the book and by offering me their criticisms or comments. They include Jacob Feldman of the Harvard School of Public Health; Raymond Illsley of the University of Aberdeen in Scotland, who was a Visiting Senior Foreign Scientist at Boston University during the 1971-72 academic year; Clara Mayo of the Psychology Department at Boston University; Martin Kozloff, a colleague in the Sociology Department at Boston University; Edgar F. Borgatta of Queens College in New York; Howard E. Freeman of the Florence Heller School at Brandeis University and the Russell Sage Foundation; and a couple of talented but anonymous reviewers. John Snyder and Theodore Sizer, then deans of the Harvard School of Public Health and the Harvard Graduate School of Education respectively, were both supportive of this research project.

I am indebted to the Maurice Falk Medical Fund and to its president, Philip Hallen, for funds for the parent interviews in 1966 and 1967 when no other funds were available for this purpose. I am also greatly appreciative of a grant from the United States Office of Education in 1967, which allowed me to undertake the research on the children in Exodus reported on in this book. Grants from the Committee on Minority Research Awards of The Social Science Research Council (1969) and from the Russell Sage Foundation (1970) were of assistance during the analysis and writing stages of this book. Neither my colleagues nor my sources of financial support are responsible for the contents of the book, however.

Jean Brady typed the first draft of the manuscript and, with Linda Feldman and Lucy Harrison, rendered valuable research assistance. I am grateful to Irene Daley both for her clerical assistance and for typing the final draft.

My debt to my wife, Ann, is great, inasmuch as she suffered through many of my research and writing problems and also contributed many valuable criticisms and comments on various parts of the manuscript as it was being prepared. I can, of course, not fail to mention my parents, Bessie and Joseph, who lovingly devoted all their lives to the care and education of their children.

LIST OF TABLES AND FIGURES

Evaluating
School Busing

THE HISTORICAL BACKGROUND
OF OPERATION EXODUS

DISTANT HISTORY: SOME SELECTED OBSER-
VATIONS ON THE EDUCATION OF
BLACKS IN BOSTON

Boston, with the largest black population in New England, was the slowest city or town in Massachusetts to provide any education at public expense for black children and was the last to provide integrated education. In 1800 a group of 66 Boston blacks, noting the absence of any provision for publicly supported education for blacks, petitioned Boston's Primary School Committee for a school for blacks, but their petition was voted down by a town meeting.[1] Not until 1820 was a separate school for blacks set up by the Primary School Committee. Several such schools were operated by the city in ensuing years. It is a well-documented fact that the schools operated for black children were the least effective of the Boston public schools. One such school, the Smith School, was judged by the Annual Visiting Committees of the Public Schools of the City of Boston in 1845 to be "the poorest of the eighteen schools visited in each of the four required grammar school studies—grammar, defi-nitions, history, and geography."[2] The Grammar School Report, submitted by Theophilus Parsons, Samuel Grideley Howe, and Rollin H. Neale, who composed the Committee on Grammar Schools, states in part:

> Your committee are aware, that there are many circum-stances to be considered before blame should be laid on any individual for the present low state of the (Smith) school. . . . But they do believe that there is good sense enough among the parents, and intellect enough among

the children, if fairly enlisted in the subject, and
directed by a zealous and discreet friend, to create a
school which shall reach at least to the rank now attained
by one half of the city schools.

It is to be regretted that the present incumbent has
not more faith in the desire of the colored population for
the education of their children; for we fear that, without
much faith, and even some enthusiasm, no great harvest
can follow the teacher's labors.[3]

Thus, saddled as they were with an ineffective grammar school
that their children were compelled to attend, it is understandable
that Boston's black parents would once again petition the Boston
School Committee on behalf of their children; they did so in 1846.
Their petition was referred to Messrs. Crowell, Kimball, Bowditch,
Ingraham, and Putnam on February 6, 1846. (Putnam shortly resigned
and was replaced by Jackson.)

The petition read:

The undersigned colored citizens of Boston, parents and
guardians of children now attending the exclusive Primary
Schools for colored children in this City, respectfully
represent; that the establishment of exclusive schools for
our children is a great injury to us, and deprives us of
those equal privileges and advantages in the public schools
to which we are entitled as citizens. These separate
schools cost more and do less for the children than other
schools, since all experience teaches that when a small
and despised class are shut out from the common benefit
of any public institutions of learning and confined to
separate schools, few or none interest themselves about
the schools—neglect ensues, abuses creep in, the standard
of scholarship degenerates, and the teachers and the
scholars are soon considered and of course become an
inferior class.

But to say nothing of any other reasons for this
change, it is sufficient to say that the establishment of
separate schools for our children is believed to be unlawful, and it is felt to be if not in intention, in fact,
insulting. If as seems to be admitted, you are violating
our rights, we simply ask you to cease doing so.

We therefore earnestly request that such exclusive
schools be abolished, and that our children be allowed to
attend the Primary Schools established in the respective
Districts in which we live.

(Signed)

George Putnam
And Eighty-five Others[4]

4

The Primary School Committee, by a three-to-two vote, rejected the petition of the black parents. The majority report claimed that most blacks preferred to attend their own separate schools and that the schools best served the blacks and whites by continuing to be separate, and reminded the blacks that they had chosen to seek separate schools rather than to attend the regular free schools.[5] The majority report also asserted that no child had the right to attend a school in its district, since it was the prerogative of the Primary School Committee to send children to schools of its choice. Further, the report claimed that, for legal purposes, the term "district" had never been defined and that Boston was one school district! The committee majority "did not believe that the law forbade the assignment of children in school according to a distinction in race or even of color, any more than of age, sex, or different degrees of attainment."[6]

The minority (Bowditch and Jackson) of the committee issued a dissenting report[7] and offered a motion that its report be printed along with the majority report. Since the motion was rejected, the minority printed its report at its own expense.

The minority report declared that it was the duty of the state to educate its rising members and that it was the right of every child in the state to receive its education at the cost of the community.[8] This report also stated that "any course on their (the Primary School Committee's) part . . . which tends to counteract, restrict, or limit, to any individual or class, the advantages and benefits designed for all, must be considered an illegal use of their authority, an arbitrary act, and exercised as illegal and arbitrary acts are, for pernicious purposes."[9] In one of its final paragraphs the report stated: "The negro pew, the Jim Crow car, and the caste school, unquestionably owe their origin to one and the same cause, and a labored effort to show this cause to be an honest regard for the best interests of the colored people should meet with the contempt which is due to gross and deliberate misrepresentation."[10] The minority members then attached letters from school administrators in Nantucket, New Bedford, Lowell, and Salem (all in Massachusetts) "to show that no injury is experienced by the Schools in those places as a consequence of educating the white and the colored children together" and that "colored children can be educated quite as well, to say the least, in the common schools as in separate schools."[11]

In 1849, having been unsuccessful in their petition to the school committee, the blacks went to court. Charles Sumner argued their case on the basis of equality before the law and the harm that segregation caused both blacks and whites.[12] The defending lawyer stressed the power of the school committee to classify students and denied inequality of services in the two systems.

5

Sumner, in his famous argument, contended that "the Courts of Massachusetts have never recognized any discrimination, founded on color or race, in the administration of the Public Schools, but have recognized the equal rights of all the inhabitants." He further stated that "the exclusion of colored children from the Public Schools, open to white children, is a source of practical inconvenience to them and their parents, to which white persons are not exposed, and is, therefore, a violation of Equality. The black and the white are not equal before the law."[13] The State Supreme Court ruled in favor of the school committee.

The final battle at that time was fought in the state legislature, which, in effect, reversed the State Supreme Court decision in the Roberts case. Criticizing the separate-school policy for its effect on residential decisions, the House Education Committee found that "even if the separate system does not force the colored parent to leave the city, it compels him, in good part, . . . to live in one section of the city, much perhaps against his convenience or pleasure."[14] The new law stated in part: "In determining the qualifications of scholars to be admitted into any public school or any district school in this Commonwealth, no distinction shall be made on account of the race, color or religious opinions, of the applicant or scholar."[15]

I have presented a very brief historical description of a battle by black parents and white supporters in a single city for improved educational opportunities for black children. Since similar battles were being fought in New York City, Cincinnati, New Haven, and other northern cities around the same time, the reader should not conclude that Boston was unique in its downgrading of black education. In slaveholding states, of course, laws had been enacted making it unlawful to teach slaves (free and slave blacks, in some cases) how to read or write. My intention in focusing on Boston is to present the reader with some knowledge of the distant background of a contemporary problem.

RECENT HISTORY: THE FORMATION OF
OPERATION EXODUS

In Boston in 1962 the local newspapers began to publish stories that reflected an apparently great concern by black parents and leaders with the quality of education that black children were receiving in Boston public schools. This concern was no doubt due to numerous factors; it is believed here that these factors included (a) the Supreme Court's School Decision of 1954, which concluded that segregated schools were unequal; (b) the oft-repeated suggestion or finding that the black children in predominantly black schools (as opposed to black children in all-black schools) were receiving an inferior education as reflected by achievement test results; and (c) an overwhelming growth in the belief by blacks that their children would need a good education if they were to compete in what was viewed as a situation of growing opportunities for blacks in the United States. This latter factor developed out of the growing strength of the civil rights movement with its strong biracial or integrated flavor.

It should be no surprise that blacks in Boston, a city long associated with liberal causes, a city that knew Crispus Attucks, William Lloyd Garrison, and Martin Luther King, would be slow in realizing or in acting on the assumption that their children might be receiving an inadequate education because they were black. So, while the sit-ins, freedom rides, and demonstrations over de jure segregation were developing in the south (with the help of northern liberals), Boston's blacks in 1960 and 1961 were slowly beginning to reassess their situation. Then, too, Boston and Massachusetts did not have segregationist laws—any segregation or discrimination practiced in schools and elsewhere was the more subtle form that was difficult to pin down. By 1962, however, blacks in northern urban settings had begun to look more closely at the way things were at home. Indeed, some of these northern blacks had originally lived in the south, and perhaps the surprise of seeing their "docile" southern brothers on the move shook them a little.

Whatever the dynamics, by 1962 the black leaders in Boston were beginning to fret about a perceived inequality in educational arrangements and opportunities for black children in their city. Boston newspaper accounts in the early 1960s revealed also that a number of black parents felt that their children were receiving an inadequate education. Black leaders and parents alike felt that teacher turnover, teacher absenteeism, infrequency or total lack of homework assignments, and overcrowded classrooms characterized the schools attended by black children and were responsible for the basic weaknesses they saw in black children's educational development. Initial concern over these conditions met with little positive response from educational officials. A brief chronology of actions beginning in 1962 and showing the concern of Roxbury blacks follows: (1) In 1962 local civil rights groups charged that de facto segregation existed in Roxbury schools. (2) In 1963, after the School Committee's repeated denials that de facto segregation existed, the first freedom stay-out (from schools) by blacks was held with 2,500 black students participating. (3) In 1964 a second school boycott was held with more that 10,000 black students (out of 25,000) participating. (4) In 1965 some of the parents began to hasten their efforts to organize the community over the situation. It is revealing to quote the remarks of one of the most articulate of these parents, who were still relatively unorganized at that time:

The problem of overcrowding in Roxbury schools became
a severe situation when parents felt frustrated and
disillusioned over the lack of communication between
themselves and administrators in seeking solutions to the
problem. Quality education is unavailable in Roxbury, not
only because of overcrowded conditions, but also because
of inadequate development of staff, outdated curriculum,
and lack of incentive in teachers for developing cre-
ativity in our children.
    We found ourselves as parents caught up in a
political maneuver between members of the Boston School
Committee and city officials who engaged in dialogue over
whether there was a "de jure" problem similar to that of
the south or a "de facto" (confined to the north) pattern in
our schools. Regardless of which phrase we adopted to
describe this disgraceful situation, we felt a severe harm
was being done to our children. This controversy over an
inadequate education and whether or not racial imbalance
exists does not happen to be a new battle. It has been
waging here since 1962.

The fact that parents were sincerely seeking a good education
for their children and that school racial integration was not their
prime concern is illustrated by this statement. It also underlines
the repeated frustrations felt by black parents when public officials
quarrel over whether or not racial imbalance exists instead of
communicating with families and addressing themselves to the real
problem as perceived by the parents: the adequacy and effectiveness
of the children's education. It is most interesting that, although few
of the parents proposed school integration for the sake of integration,
and, indeed, most of them were fearful of sending their children into
what was perceived as a hostile environment, nevertheless many of
the parents saw school integration at nonblack schools outside of
Roxbury as the only possible answer to their problem. That is, they
had no hopes that the administration of their neighborhood schools
or the quality of education in them would be immediately improved
on the basis of individual initiative. But they did believe that the
educational bureaucracy would respond both to a better organized
body of black parents and to the force to law. Consequently, in their
attempt to communicate with the educational bureaucracy, in 1965
the parents formed themselves into a voluntary association called
the "North Dorchester-Roxbury Parent Association." This association
pointed out to the educational bureaucracy the weaknesses of the
educational system vis-à-vis blacks in Boston but failed to achieve
the balanced relationship with this bureaucracy that Eugene Litwak

and Henry Meyer[16] indicate is necessary for goal achievement. Although the parent association had some power and apparently acquired allies, the educational bureaucracy remained unimpressed. Following is a sketchy outline of events that either took place at the same time or followed the formation of the parent association in Boston in 1965.

The Massachusetts State Board of Education had become concerned about the increasing number of voices raised in criticism of the inadequate educational opportunities provided for black children in Boston. It decided to deal with the issue of school racial imbalance and made possible a report on the problem prepared by the Advisory Committee on Racial Imbalance and Education.* The charge to this committee in March 1964 included an effort to determine whether or not there was racial imbalance in schools and to study both its educational consequences and ways of dealing with it if found. In brief, the Advisory Committee did find in its report dated April 1965 that racial imbalance existed in some of the communities of Massachusetts, including Boston, and that its effects were harmful. Subsequently, in August 1965, the Massachusetts legislature enacted the Massachusetts Racial Imbalance Act (Chapter 641, Acts 1965) providing for the elimination of racial imbalance in public schools, the first such state legislation in the country. The act declares it to be the policy of the Commonwealth

> to encourage all school committees to adopt as edu-
> cational objectives the promotion of racial balance and
> the correction of existing racial imbalance in the public
> schools. The prevention or elimination of racial im-
> balance shall be an objective in all decisions involving
> the drawing or altering of school attendance lines and
> the selection of new school sites. (Section 37C.)

In spite of this new state law, in spite of the influence of the Parent Association, and in spite of the evidence showing the extent of racial imbalance in Boston schools, the Boston School Committee still failed to take appropriate corrective action or even to communicate with the black Parent Association.

Indeed, the School Committee passed a proposal in midsummer of 1965 banning use of school funds for the busing of black children

----

*The Advisory Committee defined a racially imbalanced school as "one in which the racial composition of the school population is sharply out of balance with the racial composition of the society in which Negro children study, serve, and work."

to the roughly 7,000 vacant classroom seats throughout the broader Boston community. On the heels of this the superintendent of schools stated that the only feasible solution to school overcrowding was a double-session day. All of these decisions, negative ones as far as the education of Negro children is concerned, were said to be aimed at the preservation of the neighborhood school. The weakness of the neighborhood school concept, however, is the tendency of many school officials to stand behind it as a defense for inactivity in black ghettoes. Indeed, the School Committee's stand made clear to black parents, who had relied on the school authorities to educate their children, the fact that the educational system was ignoring their children's needs.

In the face of these repeated frustrations the blacks of Dorchester and Roxbury became convinced that they would have to try other problem-solving means. Mrs. Ellen Jackson, the president of the Parent Association, recalls the final events leading from the cessation of attempts to communicate with the educational bureaucracy through the mechanism of a voluntary association:

> It was because of these many affronts and confrontations with an unheeding school committee and school board that we decided that other action was necessary. After the statement by the superintendent, we called a parents' meeting at the Robert Gould Shaw House in Dorchester. Around 250 parents attended, and we discussed the problem and possible avenues to a solution. We agreed to meet nightly for a short duration, until an operative program could be mapped out. At the close of this meeting in July, 1965, there was a general consensus that a telegram should be sent to Attorney General Katzenbach seeking an injunction in order to keep this double-session day from going into effect. We also met with him several weeks later when he arrived in Boston to attend a penal convention. At this time we were assured by a man (apparently a Katzenbach assistant) who said he freely recognized the shortcomings of a double-session day, because his children had been victims of it, and that he would look into the matter.
>
> Time moved on and school was but a few weeks off. We continued to meet nightly, and attempted to arrive at a solution. We finally confined ourselves to three specific approaches to our problem. The first consisted of forming a human chain of parents around a school and

not allowing anyone to trespass. Secondly, some parents wanted to pressure more extensively, by using petitions and pickets. The third idea was to have sit-ins by parents in both classrooms and the School Committee office. Almost by a process of elimination, we voted against all three proposals because in all instances the inconvenience would be to ourselves and our children, just as in previous demonstrations, producing short-range results. We arrived at the position of mass displacement of Negro children, now called Exodus, in order to take advantage of the 7,000 vacant seats throughout the city and available under the Open Enrollment Policy. Problems arose around this decision: how to transport, and where to finance. We called a final meeting on September 8th, attended by 600 community people. At 12:30 that night, we found ourselves with 250 children to bus and with many families committed to our program. We left the meeting and embarked on a wild recruitment program to round up transportation. We called all through the night until 4 a.m., and wound up having seven buses donated by private organizations and civil rights groups. At 8 a.m. September 9, 1965, all buses, cars and children were ready to roll. The money for our buses was donated by various groups, such as the NAACP, labor unions, and from many individuals. The second day of school, we had financial support from merchants and businessmen in our immediate community. Thus, the die had been cast.

The immediate result, then, of the failure to attain satisfactory communication and action from the educational bureaucracy was change of the role of the Parent Association from that of a group attempting to establish linkage with the educational bureaucracy to a group whose chief function was one ordinarily performed by the educational bureaucracy. In the classic theory of bureaucracy this put the primary group in conflict with the bureaucracy. The parents had actually believed that they would have to run the busing operation for only a few days and that both their demonstrated concern and their taking over a function of the educational bureaucracy would so embarrass the bureaucracy that it would immediately agree to show its goodwill and intention to obey the state law on school racial imbalance by taking over the operation (and the expense) of the busing. They were wrong: four years later they were still in the busing business and receiving no aid from the educational bureaucracy of the City of Boston. Such was the birth of Operation Exodus.

The remainder of this book will deal with the author's attempt to evaluate the effects of the busing program on the children and parents involved. In the next chapter I shall describe my initial involvement with the program and then the first phase of the evaluation efforts. However, before moving on to a discussion of these early research efforts on Exodus, it might be helpful to readers if the organization were described in more detail.

In 1965, the formative year, between 300 and 400 adults were strongly involved in the Roxbury-North Dorchester Parent Association, the organization that gave rise to—and changed its name to—Operation Exodus. Mrs. Ellen Jackson, a Roxbury housewife, was chosen to be the president of the organization. Mrs. Jackson's staff indicated that some 600 adults were present on the evening of September 8, 1965, when the organization decided—in the face of School Committee opposition—to begin busing children the next day to predominantly white and uncrowded schools. The number of adults involved in this decision reflected the fact that Exodus had a broad community base, for apparently only a fraction (one-third) of these adults had school-age children. Indeed, at that time Exodus probably aroused the widest interest of any organization in the black community. One long-term resident of Roxbury said that "Exodus was the most exciting community group to come along in Roxbury in over 20 years!"

Exodus started off busing about 250 children in 1965; in 1966 the organization was busing approximately 450 children; and by 1967 it was transporting over 600 children (grades K through 10) to predominantly white schools. The bulk of these children were in grades K through 6, with larger numbers of children being bused for each of these grades than for any of the grades between 7 and 10.

The breadth of community interest was reflected in the structure of the organization, including the operating staff, the committee structure, and the board of directors. Parents, nonprofessionals in nearly every case, controlled and ran the organization. Broad policy decisions were made by the board of directors, and decisions concerning day-to-day operations were made by the office staff. Mrs. Ellen Jackson, president of the organization, was head of the office staff; Mrs. Betty Johnson was vice-president and codirector of the office staff; and Mrs. Audrey Butler was secretary of the staff. Mr. Frank Silva was treasurer. All of these staff officers were members of the board of directors. It is emphasized that the staff consisted entirely of nonprofessionals in both educational attainment and occupation.

The board of directors consisted of 25 members, with the large majority being nonprofessional. (It should be added here that the staff and board were entirely black.) Only two members of the board

of directors could claim professional status; these were Bryant
Rollins, a professional writer who was chairman of the board of
directors, and his wife, Judy, who was a schoolteacher. (I was not
elected to the board initially, having served as an informal advisor
for over a year before the board decided to extend membership to
me.)

Bryant Rollins, chairman of the board, served as head of the
organization's fundraising committee; Ralph Trotman served as head
of the bus captains committee; Mrs. Marlene McIlvaine served as
head of the school liaison committee; and Mr. Marvin Butler was
head of youth activities. Other committees included a speakers'
bureau and a community school committee, whose main function was
to help improve the neighborhood schools.

Fundraising was by all odds the most active of the committees
during the first year. The parents had never been in the school
busing business before and had had no idea of the enormous cost
involved in such an operation. Indeed, as indicated earlier, what had
begun as an operation that would likely last only a few weeks ran for
four years before any municipal or state funds were made available.
The organization, which had been granted nonprofit status, raised
and spent approximately $150,000 during the first year of its operation.
How did a group of parents, inexperienced in the nuances of educational administration and even more inexperienced in large-scale
fundraising, raise $150,000 during 1965-67? It was accomplished in
a variety of ways. Exodus first went to businessmen and shopkeepers
in the black community; these men gave generously to what they
considered a worthy cause. The organization also requested small
contributions from the parents whose children were being bused. In
addition, many whites, both in Boston and in the suburbs, formed a
fundraising group called Friends of Exodus and gave all receipts to
Exodus. Exodus also sponsored a dance during the first year and in
subsequent years and sponsored plays and concerts for the purpose
of raising funds for busing. The Exodus staff wrote program proposals
and sent applications to several foundations, some of which were
funded (e.g., Permanent Charities Foundation).

Busing costs alone during the first year amounted to over
$50,000. However, Exodus was involved in much more than busing.
The organization developed a variety of other programs during its
first year that required financial support; these included a tutorial
program, a cultural enrichment program, summer camps, a youth
recreation program, and a vocational educational program.

During the second year of its operation the organization became
more deeply involved in the development of both a Roxbury Community School Board and a private black school, the Roxbury Community School. At the same time Exodus bused even more children,

its philosophy being that busing should be available for those parents who felt that they could not wait years for the improvement of neighborhood schools but wished to meet their children's current educational needs through busing to other schools within Boston (Beacon Hill, Hyde Park, Jamaica Plain, South Dorchester, etc.). The operating expenses during the second year amounted to approximately $170,000 and during the third year to over $180,000.

In the third year of its operation the large growth in enrollment that had occurred in the second year slacked off, and by the fourth year (1968-69) the total number of children being bused had declined to approximately 500. There were probably several reasons for this. First of all, METCO, a well-supported (by federal, foundation, and state sources) operation that bused black children from Boston to cooperating suburban schools—as opposed to busing within Boston, as Exodus did—had begun to operate at the beginning of the second year of Operation Exodus. During its first year, 1966-67, METCO bused approximately 200 black children to schools in four suburban communities; during its second year METCO bused about 400 children to schools in approximately eight suburban communities. This year-to-year growth undoubtedly reflected the drawing off of many potential enrollees in the Exodus operation. After all, the Boston schools in white as well as in black neighborhoods had been criticized by many academicians as being inadequate, and it is not unreasonable to expect that some black parents would prefer to bus their children to suburban schools.

Another possible—and likely—reason for the growth decline in the Exodus enrollment during the third year concerns the development of the private black school system. By 1967 there were two private or independent schools in the black community, Highland Park Free School and The New School, and plans were under way for a third. Moreover, Exodus had taken the initiative in the development of the Roxbury Community School Board. Black parents, both those involved in Exodus and those not so involved, were primarily interested in obtaining quality education for their children, and busing was viewed as only one of the possible routes to this goal; certainly the preference of many black parents was to improve the quality of the neighborhood schools and send or keep their children in schools nearby. Thus some parents who had been busing their children via Exodus were likely to prefer sending their children to schools in the community if these were quality schools.

The development of the community private school system, then, with its attendant community control, and pushed along by the Boston School Committee's apparent opposition to any improvement of educational opportunities for black children either in the community or elsewhere, undoubtedly contributed also to the drawing off of

14

potential enrollees in Operation Exodus by the fall of 1967. It is perhaps not so paradoxical that Operation Exodus strongly encouraged and in part led the development of a black private school system in Boston's black community.*

NOTES

1. Carter G. Woodson, The Education of the Negro Prior to 1861 (New York: Arno Press and The New York Times, 1968), p. 95.

2. "Reports of the Annual Visiting Committees of the Public Schools of the City of Boston" (Boston, 1845), quoted in Robert H. Bremmer, ed., Children and Youth in America: A Documentary History (Cambridge, Mass.: Harvard University Press, 1970), I, 526.

3. Ibid., p. 527. It should be noted how similar this notion of the importance of the teacher's faith seems to Robert Rosenthal's stress on teacher expectations. See R. Rosenthal and L. Jacobson, Pygmalion in the Classroom (New York: Holt, Rinehart & Winston, 1968).

4. "Report to the Primary School Committee, June 15, 1846, on the Petition of Sundry Colored Persons for the Abolition of the Schools for Colored Children with the City Solicitor's Opinion," City Document No. 23 (Boston: City of Boston, 1846), p. 2.

5. Ibid., p. 15.

6. Ibid., p. 28.

7. "Report of the Minority of the Committee of the Primary School Board on the Caste Schools" (Boston, 1846).

8. Ibid., p. 3.

9. Ibid., p. 4.

10. Ibid., p. 19.

11. Ibid.

12. Argument of Charles Sumner, Esq., Against the Constitutionality of Separate Colored Schools in the Case of Sarah C. Roberts vs. The City of Boston (Boston, 1849), quoted in Bremmer, op. cit., p. 531.

13. Ibid.

---

*I cannot at this time go into more detail about the private black school movement; this is a complex matter. Interested readers should see a recent book dealing with this issue: Jonathan Kozol, Free Schools (Boston: Houghton Mifflin Co., 1972).

14. Report on House 167 by the Education Committee, March 1855 (Boston: General Court of Massachusetts, 1855).

15. "An Act in Amendment of 'An Act Concerning Public Schools'" (1855), Ch. 256, Massachusetts Acts and Resolves, 1854-1855 (Boston, 1855), quoted in Bremmer, op. cit., p. 535.

16. Eugene Litwak and Henry Meyer, "A Balance Theory of Coordination Between Bureaucratic Organizations and Community Primary Groups," Administrative Science Quarterly, June 1966, pp. 31-58.

2

The possibilities and value of research on the operations, problems, and consequences of Project Exodus—for the children involved, the parents, the schools, Roxbury, etc.—were readily apparent from the outset, in spite of the fact that Project Exodus came as a surprise to many people, including social scientists. Within two weeks of the project's initiation in September 1965 several local-area social scientists had briefly discussed research possibilities among themselves and had approached the Exodus leaders about the matter. Thus it was that during the latter part of September six or seven social scientists and social workers met at the office of the Northern Student Movement to plot research strategy. They had received tentative encouragement from the leaders of Operation Exodus to develop and submit their research plans to them. The social scientists came from various Boston-area universities. A second meeting followed in a week—and the boom fell. The overhasty action of one of the researchers in sending college student interviewers to approach and interview Exodus mothers and children at the bus locations, in the absence of a clear research plan and after inadequate consultation with the project leaders, resulted in the group's being told at this second meeting that research services were not desired.

Several of the social scientists, including the present author, were interested in Exodus as an action program apart from their

---

Material found in Chapter 2, pages 20-25, used by permission of Behavioral Publications, Inc., is taken largely from James E. Teele, Ellen Jackson, and Clara Mayo, <u>Family Experiences in Operation Exodus: The Busing of Negro Children</u>, Community Mental Health Journal Monograph No. 3 (1967).

research interests, and continued to be affiliated with it. My own activities were confined—voluntarily—to the problems of fundraising. Several months later I was surprised when some of the parents in the program approached me and asked if I were still interested in conducting evaluative research. When I indicated some interest, one of them, Mrs. Ellen Jackson, inquired about the nature of the research I would wish to conduct. Since I had not given the matter much thought, and since I was also aware of the parents' mixed feelings about research (although some of them felt that research could be valuable, they also felt that research often seemed pointless), I turned the question back to them and asked what questions they would like to have answered. My response piqued their interest, and they began to wonder aloud about parents' motivations for being in the program, about how well they thought their children were doing, about problems with the younger children in the first three grades, and so on. After a brief discussion it was decided that we should have a special meeting where parents and community workers would come together for the purpose of discussing the nature of research to be undertaken, if any, and related research matters such as funds, personnel, and methodology.

The ensuing meeting in December 1965 led to a decision to interview the mothers of children in the program. Although there was a strong interest in obtaining data on the experiences and performance of the children in the program, the consensus of opinion of parents at this meeting was that the children had a lot of pressure on them already and should not become research subjects. It was suggested that the parents could provide indirect data on the children's experiences at the schools to which they were being bused. It was also suggested that the present author be designated director of research. Subsequent to the meeting the staff of Operation Exodus confirmed this designation.

THE INTERVIEW AND THE INTERVIEW SCHEDULE

The other issues dealt with at the planning meeting were (1) who would do the interviewing and (2) what questions should be included in the interview schedule (influenced by our concern about questions that could be alienating and about the length of the interview). The fact that we did not have any research money and our awareness of the poor research start made in September suggested that the Exodus parents should be asked to do the interviewing. I then offered to provide training in interview-schedule design, interviewing technique, and data processing for interested parents and staff. The parents enthusiastically accepted this idea.

The other issue—what questions to include—was decided when we began to construct the interview schedule. The schedule that was developed with the assistance of parents included questions touching on the following ideas: (1) the mother's degree of satisfaction with the project and her estimate of her child's satisfaction; (2) her reason for busing her child; (3) ways in which the mother thought the operation could be improved; (4) an open-ended question on what her children said about their new school; (5) her opinion about the advisability of continuing the busing; (6) her opinion about busing the first-three-graders; (7) her prior community involvement; (8) problems she perceived regarding the Exodus program; (9) the mother's judgment and comparison of her child's performance in the prior school with performance in the new school; (10) her comparison of the amount of homework required in the previous and present schools; (11) her impression about the extent to which her child experienced or experiences prejudice or discrimination in the new school compared with the prior school; and (12) the extent to which she thinks her child benefits from attending the integrated (i.e., more balanced) school. The interview schedule also included some background and situational variables such as respondent's education, years at present residence, and number of children.

Once the interview schedule was designed the training of the interviewers began. Training sessions were held one night a week for six weeks and included discussions and evaluation of some pretests of the interview. Role-playing was included in the training of the interviewers. About ten interviewers were trained, and seven of them did the bulk of the interviewing.

THE STUDY GROUP DURING PHASE 1

Since the majority of the children bused by Exodus were attending elementary grades 1 through 6, and since interest was focused on the first six grades, the sample was restricted accordingly. Families having children only in kindergarten and/or junior high school were not included in the group designated for interviewing, even though such children were bused as a part of the Exodus program. However, if the family had children in kindergarten or junior high school bused by Exodus in addition to a child in one of the first six grades, then the family was included in our target group. These procedures produced a target group of 126 mothers with whom interviews were attempted. Of these, 103 mothers, or 82 percent, were successfully interviewed. There were no direct refusals by those not interviewed; they either were not at home on repeated visits or failed to keep several appointments with interviewers. The

103 mothers had a total of 221 children in Exodus. While most of the tabulations presented later are based on the number of mothers interviewed, we also present some data based on the number of children these women had in Exodus. No information was collected on those not interviewed; hence we cannot comment on possible differences between them and those interviewed.

The interviewing began during the last week of February and was largely completed by early April 1966. However, because of the many competing demands on the interviewers' time, such as helping to raise money with which to keep the buses rolling, about one-third of the interviews were not completed until June. Comparison of the data from the earlier and later interviews revealed no substantial differences between the two groups.

RESULTS OF THE EARLY RESEARCH

As indicated earlier with respect to the initial research effort, we were interested in obtaining data on the parents' motivations, attitudes, and experiences with the program; we were also interested in obtaining data on family structure, residential stability, and educational background of the parents involved. At that time we were not focusing on the tasks of evaluation and explanation. The researchers wanted primarily to be able to describe what was going on, what was being perceived by parents (including their reports on the children's feelings), and the parents' stated attitudes and motivations. It was understood by the researchers that later experiences of the children if observed by researchers, the expansion of the research design to include the addition of a control group, and observations on the teachers and others involved in the experience might enable us or others to lengthen and broaden the process to the extent that evaluation and explanation could be attempted. So the findings from the first phase of the research are purely descriptive, despite the fact that at times some variables were treated as independent variables and others as dependent ones. For the convenience of the reader a few of these early findings are presented here, although a fuller report on them has already been presented elsewhere.[1]

In Table 1 we present the results of an attempt to find out how the mothers came to hear about the plans for the busing operation.

Essentially the responses to the question "How did you hear about Operation Exodus?" reveal that the largest proportion of the mothers helped to formulate the project themselves or heard about it firsthand from a friend. The success of Exodus in sustaining the busing operation is probably due in large measure to this initially large organizational base. From the beginning, apparently, there

TABLE 1

Distribution of Responses to the Question
"How did you hear about Operation Exodus?"

Response Category	N	Percent
Read in newspaper	4	4.0
Read in leaflets	6	5.8
Heard on radio	9	8.7
Heard on TV	5	4.9
Heard from friend	37	35.9
Helped formulate project	39	37.9
Other	3	2.8
Total	103	100.0

was widespread community interest among Roxbury's black mothers, a fact that gave its designated leadership a powerful voice in the community.

Motivations

We were more interested, however, in the mothers' motivations for sending their children, some of them young, on buses to schools in predominantly white neighborhoods of Boston, in view of the controversy being waged over busing within both the white and black communities. Informal discussions held with the leaders of Operation Exodus and with other community leaders in 1965 revealed that many of them were concerned about the potential dangers in busing the black children into white neighborhoods.* In the white community Mrs. Louise Day Hicks, vocal chairman of the Boston School Committee, led the outcry against busing "little Negro children" into white schools; her battle cry was "save the neighborhood school." She was apparently responding to the objection of whites in Boston to school racial integration.

In response to our question "Why did you bus your child(ren)?" an overwhelming majority of Exodus respondents (86 percent) indicated

---

*A danger subsequently revealed to its fullest extent in South Carolina, New Orleans, Canarsie, and elsewhere.

21

that only a desire for a better educational opportunity for their children had motivated them. More specifically, they mentioned overcrowding, lack of individual attention, and delapidated facilities as intolerable conditions in the Roxbury schools. Only 7 percent of the mothers indicated that a desire to have the children attend an integrated school motivated them. (No information on this item was obtained from the remaining 7 percent.) As indicated, this was an open-ended question, and the mothers could have included both reasons (quality education and school integration) in their response. Being somewhat surprised by the distribution of responses to this question, we decided to examine the responses to a question designed to elicit the extent to which the mothers had been involved in prior educational activities. It was found that 80 percent of the respondents had participated previously in some educational activity on behalf of their children. Many of these parents had been involved in one or more of the following activities: Headstart, tutorial programs, and school strikes. It would seem, then, that the respondents may be characterized as having been at the outset of the busing operation more interested in the particular educational success of their children than in the pursuit of school integration, though to be sure these two goals may have been related in the minds of some of them. Put another way, it would seem that parents' concern over the apparently inadequate and destructive educational experiences their children were receiving in their community schools, along with the lack of constructive response on the part of school authorities overrode the fears they may have had about busing young children into pre-dominantly white neighborhoods.

Level of Satisfaction with the Program

Next we present the frequency distribution of responses to several related questions that may be characterized as evaluative: (1) "How satisfied are you with the Exodus busing program?" (2) "Do you want this type of transfer of children to continue?" (3) "What suggestions do you have for improvement of the program?" The first of these questions was precoded as indicated in Table 2. The others were open-ended, and responses were later categorized as indicated in Table 3. Where the number of responses do not add up to 103 the difference is due to lack of information on the item.

It is not surprising that the respondents indicate a quite general satisfaction with the Exodus Program and that they would want to see the busing continued during the following year. Hence we had a considerable interest in the responses to the question calling for suggestions for ways in which the program—including the busing—might be improved.

Almost half of the mothers did have suggestions for improvement, and 30 percent had suggestions dealing with the busing operation specifically. Primarily these mothers seemed interested in maintaining behavior controls on the buses or in having the buses operate more efficiently.

Although we did not interview the children during the first year of the program, we did ask the mothers about their children's impressions of the busing and their new school experiences. As indicated, the 103 mothers had a total of 221 children in the program. The following proportions of children were said by the mothers to be very satisfied, fairly well satisfied, and dissatisfied: 76.7, 17.8,

TABLE 2

Frequency Distributions on Selected Variables (N=103)

Variable	N	Percent
1. Satisfaction of parents in Exodus		
Very satisfied	80	77.7
Fairly well satisfied	16	15.5
Not satisfied	7	6.8
2. Want the busing to continue?		
Yes, without reservation	91	94.8
Yes, with reservation	5	5.2
3. Suggestions for improvement		
Mother satisfied, no suggestions for improvement	52	53.6
Better behavior control needed on bus	15	15.5
Need more parental cooperation in program	11	11.3
Need a more efficient bus service	8	8.3
Retain same drivers on bus routes	6	6.2
Need coordination between Exodus and the schools	1	1.0
Plans for continuing new student friendship bonds outside school	1	1.0
Provision of nursing service so more mothers can aid Exodus	1	1.0
Need more widespread participation of neighborhood's children	2	2.1

and 1.4 percent respectively. For the remaining 4.1 percent (13 children) the mothers indicated lack of knowledge about the children's evaluation. All in all, then, the mothers reported that they and their children were generally satisfied with the operation, though it is notable that the mothers carefully indicated the areas in which they thought improvements could be made. Since they were in constant communication with the Exodus headquarters, it is understandable that they reported their concerns to Ellen Jackson and her staff as they arose, and that subsequently many of their suggestions—such as keeping the same drivers on given routes—were acted upon during the course of the first year's operation.

Busing of Children in First Three Grades

This is the last of our findings from phase 1 to be presented here. As indicated earlier, one of the issues of paramount concern to the Exodus leaders as well as to educational leaders in the city and state had to do with the advisability of busing the first-three-graders. Although several distinguished social scientists (Thomas Pettigrew, J. K. Morland, and M. Goodman)[2] have suggested problematic areas in the desegregation process that cry out for research, it is a shock to find that even with respect to desegregation in the south little is known about the relative advantages and disadvantages of initiating the process among children at various grade levels. Generally speaking, opinion appears divided on the issue. Southern educators appear to favor beginning the desegregation process in the highest grade, i.e., the senior year in high school. Black leaders seem to lean toward the initiation of desegregation in the lower grades. If the goal is to reduce susceptibility to prejudice, the weight of our knowledge about the socialization processes would seem to favor desegregation at the lower grades. Nevertheless, the studies of Morland, Goodman, and Kenneth Clark inform us that race prejudice and preference are discernible in children as young as three or four years of age.[3] Robert Coles has also dealt with the devastating reactions to participating in the school desegregation process among young black children.[4] Still, all too little is known about the age-specific reactions of either black or white children (and their parents) to desegregation in the South.

Even less is known about this issue in northern areas, where it is clouded by de facto as opposed to de jure segregation. Because of the controversy welling up in Boston around the busing of very young children the mothers were asked, "How do you feel about busing the first-three-graders?" Responses were then coded and placed in one of the following three categories: (1) strongly in favor of busing first-three-graders, (2) in favor but with reservations, and (3) strongly opposed to busing first-three-graders.

Only 9 percent of the mothers were opposed to busing the first-three-graders; 31 percent were in favor but with reservations; while 60 percent were unreservedly in favor of busing the first-three-graders. Of those opposed four said that the young children "required too much supervision," two felt that the younger children "can't take care of themselves," and one said the younger children should "attend school closer to home." Typical among those in favor of busing younger children but having reservations about it was the mother who said that "under the circumstances (of conditions in Roxbury schools) I am in favor of busing the younger children if it means a superior education, though I am wary of it." An interesting difference appeared when we crosstabulated opinions about busing first-three-graders with whether or not the parent had a child in one of the first three grades. This differences is shown in Table 3.

Clearly, the relationship is a substantial one (being statistically significant at the .01 level) and shows that those more in favor of busing first-three-graders have such a child, while those less inclined to busing the younger children do not have any first-three-graders in the program. A closer examination of the data shows that only eight respondents definitely opposed busing the first three grades and that six of the eight did not have a child in one of the first three grades. Thus those who are in the best position to know the problems involved in busing the younger children are also most in favor of it. We believe this finding is related to the very favorable and satisfying experiences that the children in the first three grades were having. It is true, of course, that the respondents with first-three-graders are younger, and their youth probably makes them more willing to face the additional challenge of busing younger children. Such variable interaction, however, does not alter the basic fact that those who have younger children are also more willing to see them bused.

Feedback of Results

These findings, along with others from the first-year research, are more fully reported elsewhere.[5] They were reported first, of course, to the parents in Operation Exodus, who were extremely eager to utilize them in their program planning. Indeed, Mrs. Ellen Jackson was a co-author of the first published report on Exodus.

Apparently the parents found these largely descriptive findings useful in attempting not only to improve their busing program but to meet more specific educational needs of the children, such as the need for tutorial assistance and educational counseling. By the

TABLE 3

Grade Category and Busing Children in
Lower Grades (N=84)*

	Respondent's Opinion on Busing Lower Grade Children						
Does family have child in one of first 3 grades?	Thinks should be bused		Yes, but with reservations		Should not be bused		100%=
	N	Percent	N	Percent	N	Percent	
YES	41	71.9	14	24.6	2	3.5	57
NO	8	29.6	13	48.2	6	22.2	27

*Insufficient information in 19 cases.

rpbs = .40 P < .01

end of the first year of the program the Exodus staff had already begun to lay the groundwork for the establishment of tutorial programs, a psychological counseling service, and a recreational program, all of which had appeared as suggestions from parents interviewed in our study. The staff had moved into remodeled quarters, completed by the fathers in Exodus, which were large enough to hold these expanded educational services. Indeed, there apparently was never a second thought about whether the busing program was going to run a second year once it became clear that the parents approved of the program. Similarly, the leaders of the program automatically assumed that the research would continue and so informed the present author.

THE SECOND-YEAR RESEARCH

Thus interviews were held with 78 new parents who enrolled their children in the program for the first time just prior to its second year, 1966-67. In addition a sample (25 percent) of veteran parents from the first year were reinterviewed during the second year of the research, and interviews were completed during the fall of 1966. Some results of the second-year research have been published elsewhere.[6] Responses from second-year parents supported or confirmed impressions gained on the basis of the first year's study with respect to motivation for busing, satisfaction with the program, problems with the program, and the like. The reader will recall, for example, that we reported that 86 percent of the first-year Exodus parents indicated that they were motivated primarily by the desire for better educational opportunities for their children. Among second-year enrollees 89 percent gave this as their reason for busing.

However, an interesting thing happened during the fall of the 1966-67 school year. The leaders of Operation Exodus began to grow curious about the children's experiences, behavior, and performance in school and indicated that they wished to know more about these matters from the children's perspective. The Exodus staff indicated that they would welcome the development of an expanded research program provided the author continued to direct the research.

A variety of considerations apparently entered into the staff's willingness to consider research involving the children in Exodus. Probably foremost among these was their very real concern about the children's academic performance; they felt they needed some kind of systematic measure of the children's academic progress and they were not getting this from either the school system or the children's parents. Experience had shown that many parents failed for one reason or another to report their children's school performance to the Exodus office, even when forms were provided for this. In addition the school superintendent (probably under instruction of the School Committee) had refused to provide the research team with either academic data or access to school records on the children in Exodus.

Another reason for the Exodus staff's interest in an expanded research study had to do with their fundraising efforts. They had come to realize that granting organizations, including the federal government, when asked to contribute operating funds would invariably request facts and evaluative data concerning the children's progress.

Still another reason, perhaps, was the fact that the Exodus staff had come to know those conducting research on Exodus and to respect their judgment and integrity. Perhaps, too, the participation by some of the parents in the development of the interview schedule as well as in the actual interviewing had helped instill in them an appreciation for the research process. In any event, in the fall of 1966 I was asked to develop a research plan that would answer some of the questions then being raised by blacks—within and outside of Exodus—about the value of this particular school integration program. I developed a research proposal, evaluative in nature, during the winter of 1966-67 and submitted it through Harvard University, with which I was then affiliated, to the United States Office of Education in January 1967. This proposal, calling for evaluative research to be conducted during the 1967-68 school year, was approved and funded by the Office of Education. Essential aspects of this design, described earlier as phase 2 of the research and as the core of the evaluation I attempted on Operation Exodus, are presented in the next chapter.

NOTES

1. See James E. Teele, Ellen Jackson, and Clara Mayo, Family Experiences in Operation Exodus: The Bussing of Negro Children, Community Mental Health Journal Monograph No. 3 (New York: Columbia University Press, 1967).

2. Thomas F. Pettigrew, "Social Psychology and Desegregation Research," in I. Steiner and M. Fishbein (eds.), Current Studies in Social Psychology (New York: Holt, Rinehart and Winston, 1965); J. K. Morland, "A Comparison of Race Awareness in Northern and Southern Children," American Journal of Orthopsychiatry, XXXVI (1966), 22-31; M. Goodman, Race Awareness in Young Children, Rev. ed. (New York: Collier, 1964).

3. Kenneth Clark, Prejudice and Your Child (Boston: Beacon Press, 1963); Morland, op. cit.; Goodman, op. cit.

4. Robert Coles, The Desegregation of Southern Schools: A Psychiatric Study (New York: Anti-Defamation League of B'nai B'rith and Atlanta: Southern Regional Council, 1963).

5. Teele, Jackson, and Mayo, op. cit.

6. James E. Teele and Clara Mayo, "School Racial Integration: Tumult and Shame," Journal of Social Issues, XXV, 1 (January 1969), 137-156.

It was intended that phase 2 of the research on Operation Exodus would concentrate on the new group of children who would be joining the program in September 1967. Since the research to be conducted involved departures from past practices in the type of study group, data collection technique, and research aims, I have referred to this as the second phase of the research conducted on Operation Exodus.

The basic design called for the following:

1. A "before-after" study (a quasi-experimental design) involving about 250 students in grades 3-6 who were participating in Exodus for the first time beginning in September 1967. These students were to be compared at two points in time, spanning a school year with an appropriate group of 250 non-Exodus black students still in attendance at the predominantly black neighborhood schools, on measures of social adjustment, achievement, self-perception, and attitudes toward learning and control of environment. Parental characteristics, parental attitudes, socioeconomic factors, and school characteristics were to be utilized as control variables.

2. A continuing study of the children in grades 3-6 who had begun their participation in Exodus in either September 1965 or September 1966. This it was thought would permit some kind of comparison of achievement scores, achievement change, and school adjustment between new and experienced Exodus children.

3. Continuing assessment of attitude changes among 200 current Exodus mothers and later comparisons with 100 new Exodus mothers and 100 non-Exodus mothers. The major focus however was to be on the experimental aspects described in 1.

The major hypotheses were as follows:

1. Exodus children will show more positive change in achievement and in attitudes than non-Exodus children.

2. The more accepting Exodus children feel their teachers and classmates are of them, the greater the positive change in achievement.

3. Among Exodus children who feel accepted a direct relationship will exist between proportion of white classmates and positive change in achievement.

The basic aspects of the research as it was planned are presented in the remainder of this chapter. Changes that were necessitated in the implementation phase are presented in subsequent chapters.

THE RESEARCH PROBLEM

The major emphasis of the research was to be on (1) whether or not the children who were bused gained more than those not bused on measures of achievement and self-image, and (2) the factors related to academic achievement of the children in Project Exodus. The "explanatory" factors on which data was collected fell within the following domains: (1) child's attitudes, (2) classroom factors, and (3) background characteristics of the child and his family. At the beginning of the school year, what factors differentiate the children who participated in Project Exodus from a comparison group of black children who did not participate? At the end of the school year, did the children who participated in Exodus show greater gains than a comparison group of non-Exodus children in achievement (as indexed by tests of reading ability), in getting along with peers, in the acquisition of a positive self-concept, in acquiring feelings of mastery over the environment, in the development of interest in school and reading? Similarly, what factors (social and personality) differentiated the mothers who sent their children to schools in the Exodus program from those who did not? Were the Exodus mothers likelier than the non-Exodus mothers to believe that their neighborhood schools were overcrowded and inadequate and that their children could get a better education in the predominantly white public schools in Boston? Were the Exodus mothers likelier to have a pioneering spirit and to believe in their ability to influence events? Did the Exodus mothers have a more accepting view of integration than non-Exodus mothers? In which group of mothers did the greatest attitudinal changes take place? What effects did maternal attitudes and attitudinal changes appear to have on the children's school performance? What effects did the racial composition of the classroom have on academic and social achievement? These were some of the questions the research had hoped to answer. The questions obviously relate to several specific areas of interest: (1) the Exodus children's performance in comparison to non-Exodus children; (2) the social and personality characteristics and attitudes of Exodus and non-Exodus mothers; (3) the relationship among maternal characteristics, child's attitudes, and the child's school performance; (4) the relationship of school and classroom factors to school performance. Prior research that was relevant to the study at that point in time (1967) is discussed in the following section.

PRIOR RELEVANT RESEARCH

The report by James Coleman and his associates[1] was the most recent and certainly the most comprehensive research dealing with aspects of many of the problems considered in the research on Exodus. More specifically, the Coleman report dealt with the following areas that appeared to be the most relevant to the proposed research: (1) the relationship of school racial composition to academic achievement for Negro and white children; (2) the relationship of family background characteristics to academic achievement; (3) the relationship of the children's attitudes and feelings to academic achievement. A thoughtful report by Irwin Katz[2] was highly relevant, particularly his consideration of the importance of the children's attitudes, feelings, and motivations. A report by Alan Wilson[3] was especially pertinent to the consideration of the relationship between school racial composition and academic achievement, since it focused on aspirations.

Wilson's was one of the first systematic investigations of the relationship between student-body characteristics and educational outcomes. In a study of the relationship between attendance at social class-integrated schools and aspirations to attend college and to attain professional employment, Wilson found that both aspirations were severely restricted among boys attending predominantly "working-class" schools in contrast to boys in predominantly "white-collar" schools. This finding, incidentally, holds when the social status of the family—indexed by father's occupation and parental educational level—is held constant. Thus, when the sons of professionals attended a "high-class" school 93 percent of them wished to attend college, but when the sons of professionals attended a "working-class" school only 64 percent wished to attend college. For the sons of manual workers the comparable proportions were 59 percent and 33 percent. Furthermore, when grades or IQ's are held constant, substantially more of the students receiving the same grade in the "high-class" schools want to attend college. Clearly, then, the school's atmosphere was as important as social class in influencing a boy to attend college. Wilson concluded that "the de facto segregation brought about by concentration of social classes in cities results in schools with unequal morale climates which likewise affect the motivation of the child, not necessarily by inculcating a sense of inferiority, but rather by providing a different ethos in which to perceive values."[4]

Findings by Coleman and his associates appear to support as well as extend the findings of Wilson. Coleman and his colleagues found that as the proportion of white students increases in a school achievement among black students increases, apparently because of the association between white ethnicity and social-class factors. These authors also reported that school facilities and curricula and teacher characteristics accounted for less variation in the achievement of minority-group children than did attributes of other students.

However, since Coleman and his associates collected their data at a single point in time, they were unable to deal prospectively with the ways in which changes in environment might be related to changes in attitudes and in achievement scores. They did present data to show that black ninth-graders with the longest experience of integrated schooling had a much higher achievement score than black ninth-graders who had never had white classmates, which suggested that changes in achievement might result from the attendance of black students at schools that contain a high proportion of white students. It was felt that the utilization of an experimental design in the research on Operation Exodus would permit the assessment of changes in achievement and other factors that resulted from the attendance of black children in predominantly white schools in Boston.

Another explanatory variable that had been emphasized in a variety of studies and which was considered highly relevant to the study of Exodus was "sense of mastery of the environment." V. C. Crandall, et al.,[5] Katz,[6] and Coleman and his associates have all presented findings suggesting that whether a person believes that his own efforts determine his external rewards will strongly affect his perception of the attractiveness or value of a given achievement goal as well as his expectation of success. In the Coleman study three expressions of student attitude and motivation were measured and examined in relation to achievement. These attitudes, which are quite similar to the factors mentioned by Katz as being related to achievement, are (1) interest in schoolwork and reading outside of school, (2) self-concept with respect to learning and success in school, and (3) sense of control of own fate. Coleman and his associates report that "of all the variables in the survey, including all measures of family background and all school variables, these attitudes showed the strongest relation to achievement at all three grade levels [grades 6, 9, and 12]."[7]

Coleman's findings on the variables that pertain to black students are most suggestive. Black students (except occasionally Oriental Americans) were the most likely to report high interest in learning, indexed by (a) proportion reporting that they wanted to be among the best in class, (b) proportion who report studying outside of school, and (c) proportion staying away from school because they didn't want to come. Coleman had found, however, that this interest of black students in learning was not translated into effective learning. To get an idea as to why this was the case Coleman examined closely the relationship between sense of control of own fate and achievement. To assess sense of fate control students were asked to respond to three statements: "good luck is more important than hard work for success," "every time I try to get ahead something or somebody stops me," and "people like me don't have much of a chance to be successful in life." Only a small fraction of the variance in sense of fate control was accounted for by family background factors and almost none of it by objective school characteristics.* The sense of fate control accounted for about three times as much variance in the test scores of blacks as of whites, and for blacks was the most important of the three attitudes. Coleman clearly states that this relationship does not imply the causal sequence and that in fact it may be two-directional.

Still, Coleman and his associates did make an attempt to explain their findings. They included the fact that achievement by white students in contrast to that of blacks was more closely related to self-concept than to control of environment. In the words of the Coleman report, "For children from advantaged groups, achievement or lack of it appears closely related to their self-concept: what they believe about themselves. For children from disadvantaged groups, achievement or lack of achievement appears closely related to what they believe about their environment: whether they believe the environment will respond . . . or whether they believe it is . . . immovable."[8] The importance of the belief about the environment in determining level of performance is suggested by the the finding that black pupils who answered "hard work" to the first question scored higher on a test of verbal ability than did white pupils who chose the "good luck" response.

In view of the findings of Crandall, of Katz, and especially those of Coleman and his associates it was decided that data bearing on

---

*However, as the proportion of whites in school increased the black child's sense of internal control increased.

the relationship between these attitudes and later changes in achievement scores would be collected.

PARENTAL FACTORS AND ATTITUDES OF CHILDREN

Coleman notes[9] that unpublished research by Roberta Bear, Robert Hess, and Virginia Shipman on black mothers and their four-year-old children in Chicago shows that those mothers with a sense of futility relative to the environment have children with lower scores on Stanford-Binet IQ tests, after other aspects of the mother's behavior, including her own IQ score, are statistically controlled. Later on, in connection with the discussion of the genesis of attitudes, Coleman suggests that school integration may be related to the development of these attitudes (self-concept, interest in learning, fate control) in minority-group children.* However, Coleman also states that "it appears reasonable that these attitudes depend more on the home than the school," and adds that "such inquiry into the source of these attitudes can best be carried out by such intensive studies on a smaller scale than the present survey."[10] Thus it was felt that additional interviews with the study children's mothers should be conducted. (Indeed, earlier research results based on interviews with the mothers of Exodus have already been referred to in Chapter 2.[11]) Based on data collected from both mother and child, I planned to assess the relationships between, on the one hand, maternal personality characteristics, maternal attitudes toward education and integration, background of the parents, and the structure of the home, and, on the other hand, the child's attitudes, the child's achievement score, and changes in the child's attitudes and achievement score.** In addition, an extensive analysis of the differences between the mothers of Exodus and of non-Exodus children was planned. Two of the factors

---

*Tangentially, Eugene Weinstein and Paul Geisel found alienation of mothers, indexed by Srole's Anomia Scale, to be strongly related to the mother's decision to send her child to a desegregated school in Nashville. These authors also found a direct relationship between pioneering and desegregation. See "Family Decision Making Over Desegregation," Sociometry, March 1962, pp. 21-29.

**In a relevant research report Maxwell Schleifer and James Teele in an unpublished study of school dropouts and nondropouts in a lower-class neighborhood in Cambridge found that the mothers of dropouts had more negative attitudes toward education and lower aspirations for their children. This paper, entitled "The Mothers of School Dropouts: Alienated Adults," was presented at the Massachusetts Conference on Social Welfare, 1964.

to be included in this analysis were mother's aspirations for her child and mother's changes in attitudes. It was expected that the data to be gathered on the mothers in September 1967 (this will be discussed more fully in the section on METHOD) would serve not only as baseline data for mothers who would be reinterviewed later on but would also be the source of independent or predictor variables with regard to changes in the children's academic achievement and social behavior.

SOCIAL ADJUSTMENT OF THE CHILDREN AT SCHOOL

Data on the social adjustment of Exodus and non-Exodus children at school was also collected during the study. The children were asked questions designed to tap the extent to which they had white and nonwhite friends, felt accepted by their classmates, felt that their teachers approved of them, and so on. Studies by Katz and James McPartland had suggested the salience of these factors. Katz[12] found that college-level blacks perform much better in test situations when they receive approval from the tester but noted that no studies of this kind have been performed on students below the college level. Summarizing some of the relevant work done in this area, Katz suggests that special attention should be given to the distinction between the racially integrated classroom in which the minority child experiences acceptance and the merely desegregated classroom where he feels unwelcome. Although Coleman says little on this point, Katz reports that "further unpublished analyses of the Coleman data by James McPartland reveal the expected difference between truly integrated and merely desegregated schools. Those schools with more than half white student bodies whose Negroes score well, when compared with similar schools whose Negroes score poorly, are characterized by greater cross-racial acceptance as predicted. Their students were much more likely to report close friends among members of the other race than students in the merely desegregated schools."[13] Thus it was hoped that in the present study similar comparisons could be made between schools where cross-racial acceptance was high and schools where cross-racial acceptance was low. Moreover, following up the earlier study of the mothers in Exodus, it was hoped that assessments could be made of the relationship between the Exodus mother's estimate of her child's acceptance at school and the child's school performance. More specifically, in the earlier study an inverse relationship was found between the mother's estimate of the prejudice her child encountered and the mother's judgment of the benefits of attending an integrated school.[14]

HYPOTHESES

It was anticipated that the research design would permit an opportunity for the assessment of changes over at least one school year, and in some cases even longer. Based on prior research and theory, the main hypothesis of the proposed research was that changes in reading achievement of the Exodus children would be greater than for non-Exodus children. Among the Exodus children, however, it was anticipated that those who attended schools characterized by an accepting atmosphere would progress more than those who did not attend such schools.

Consistent with findings by Coleman and his colleagues as well as by others, it was also anticipated that the proportion of white students in class with Exodus and non-Exodus black children would be related to changes in achievement for black children. It was further expected, however, that this would more likely be the case when the black children experienced feelings of acceptance from teachers and classmates.

It was also believed, consistent with J. Rotter's[15] and Coleman's[16] findings on sense of personal control over the environment, that those children who came from families that had high aspirations for the children would be likelier to have children who believed that they could influence events. Such children, it was anticipated, would have greater gains in achievement than children who did not have a sense of fate control.

It had been found by L. Srole[17] and numerous other researchers that adults who lacked a sense of control, i.e., were alienated as indexed by Srole's Anomia Scale, were also likely to be authoritarian and rigid. Thus some of Srole's personality scales were included in the parent-interview schedule on the hunch that authoritarian and/or alienated parents might retard the development of children in school.[18] The reasoning here was that the strength and direction of parental feelings and beliefs might be directly related to the child's learning through rewards and punishments, in much the same way that teachers are believed to directly affect learning. Crandall, et al.,[19] and B. Rosen and R. C. D'Andrade[20] are among those reporting on the relationship between maternal approval and children's achievement striving.

The change hypotheses that guided the study are listed below. All hypotheses stated here applied only to new Exodus parents and children, participating for the first time in 1967, and to the comparison group of non-Exodus parents and children.

1. Exodus children will show more positive change in achievement than non-Exodus children.

2. Exodus as well as non-Exodus children who have a sense of control of own fate will show more positive change in achievement than will children who do not have a sense of fate control.

3. In both Exodus and non-Exodus families, mothers who are not authoritarian and not anomic (i.e., do not lack a sense of fate control) are more likely to have children who show positive change in achievement than are authoritarian and anomic mothers. (In the explication of hypotheses 1, 2, and 3, analysis of interaction among parental attitudes, child's attitudes, and achievement changes is planned separately for Exodus and for non-Exodus children.)

4. The more accepting Exodus children feel their teachers and classmates are of them, the greater the positive change in achievement.

5. Among Exodus children who feel accepted, a direct relationship will exist between proportion of white classmates and positive change in achievement. The opposite relationship will hold for Exodus children who do not feel accepted.

With respect to the last hypothesis it was emphasized that it was not expected that all Exodus children would improve or that none of the non-Exodus children would show changes in desired directions. What was hoped was that the study would allow the researcher to explain changes among both the Exodus and the non-Exodus children. It was felt that if some of the non-Exodus children showed improved attitudes and test scores, it should be possible to indicate the factors related to doing well in non-Exodus, i.e., predominantly black schools. It was also hoped that home and school and child factors related to doing well (and to not doing well) could be isolated.

METHOD

The Primary Study Groups

The Exodus Study Group

Since the main emphasis in the study was to be the comparison of Exodus and non-Exodus children from grades 3 through 6, the design called for school surveys and achievement tests of all new Exodus children entering grades 3 through 6 in September 1967, and in May 1968 as well as for a control group of children of the same grade level but attending racially-imbalanced schools in the black community. These two groups of children were to be the main focus of the before-after study. The mothers of the new Exodus children as well as the mothers of the comparison group of non-Exodus children were to be interviewed at the beginning of the school year (September) and again in May, near the end of the school year. It was estimated, based on previous experience in Exodus, that approximately 100 mothers would register their children in the Exodus program in grades 3-6 for the first time in the summer of 1967. The staff of Operation Exodus had indicated to the principal investigator that this number of new parents and their children (approximately 250) would be enrolled by mid-August. It was thus expected by the investigator that the task of securing the control group of non-Exodus families would commence in early August.

The Control Group

The plan was that once the children's names, previous schools attended, and previous grades attended were obtained from the Exodus office, these data would be submitted to the office of the Boston school superintendent. The superintendent's office had promised the investigator that it would supply the name and address of the child adjacent on a classroom list to each Exodus child at the sending school, that is, at the last predominantly black school attended by the new Exodus enrollee. The investigator would then contact the parents of the adjacent non-Exodus child and, after explaining the nature of the study, request that they and their child participate in the research study. Since there were two children adjacent to each Exodus child on the list, we would have a control group equal in number to the Exodus group if the parents of only one of each pair of adjacent children decided to participate in the study. It was expected that the interviewing of non-Exodus parents would be completed by mid-September 1967 and that the non-Exodus children would be surveyed and tested during the latter part of September.

Assuming that a non-Exodus child and parent would be secured (but not matched) for each Exodus child and parent, the primary study group would consist of 500 children and 200 parents (predominantly mothers).

The Secondary Study Group

As Exodus would be entering its third year of operation in September 1967, there would be about 200 children, grades 3 through

6, and about 150 mothers with previous experience in Operation
Exodus. The experienced Exodus mothers had already been inter-
viewed once near the beginning of their children's involvement in
Exodus. It was planned to reinterview these mothers in August 1967.
Moreover, since none of the children with previous experience in
Exodus had been surveyed, we planned to test and survey them in
September 1967 along with the new Exodus and the non-Exodus chil-
dren, focusing, of course, only on children in grades 3 through 6.
All of the Exodus children from all three years and the non-Exodus
children would then be administered a second achievement test in
June 1968 along with a short survey questionnaire. No comparison
group of non-Exodus children was to be drawn for the experienced
Exodus children.

Instruments

Parents

For both sets of parents, new Exodus and non-Exodus, two
interviews were planned and conducted, one at the beginning of the
school year and one at the end of the school year. Baseline and pred-
ictive data, such as measures of personality characteristics, were
gathered during the first interview, and effect data, such as attitudes
toward integration and perception of their child's school performance,
were gathered during the second interview. Some of the attitudinal
data were collected at both points in time in order that attitude changes
might be assessed.

Children

An appropriate reading achievement test, the Metropolitan
Reading Subtest, was administered to both Exodus and non-Exodus
children in the study.
School questionnaires were also administered to both Exodus
and non-Exodus children at the beginning and at the end of the school
year. A copy of the first-stage questionnaire administered to all
third- and fourth-graders, Exodus and non-Exodus, is attached as
Appendix A. In addition, a copy of the first-stage questionnaire
administered to all fifth- and sixth-grade students is attached as
Appendix B. These questionnaires were pretested during the spring
of 1967.

TABLE 4

Data Collected: Baseline and Post Data

Areas of Research	Mothers		Children	
	Exodus	Non-Exodus	Exodus	Non-Exodus
I. Personality characteristics: self-image, alienation, authoritarianism, rigidity, frustration, etc.	+	+	-	-
II. Attitudes towards:				
1. Civil rights	+	+	-	-
2. Desegregation of schools	+	+	-	-
3. Quality education	+	+	-	-
4. Integration of schools	+	+	-	-
5. Civil liberties	+	+	-	-
6. Pioneering in desegregation	+	+	-	-
7. Self, learning and control of environment	-	-	+	+
8. Teachers and the school	+	+	+	+
III. School performance and adjustment of children's and mother's perception of school experience:				
Achievement	+	+	+	+
Attendance	+	+	+	+
Cross-racial friendships	+	+	+	+
IV. Community participation				
Social isolation scale	+	+	-	-
Attitude towards neighborhood	+	+	-	-
V. Background variables (parents)				
Ethnicity	+	+	+	+
Age	+	+	+	+
Class (occupation and education)	+	+	-	-
Place of birth	+	+	-	-
Years at present residence	+	+	-	-
VI. Educational and occupational aspirations for the children	+	+	+	+

Interviewers

Professional social workers and several of the parents who were trained during the early research (phase 1) directed by the present author were employed as interviewers. Those interviewers who had not previously worked on Exodus research were trained in interviewing procedures by the principal investigator and his staff.

Testers

The testers, chosen by the investigator, were all experienced teachers. These teachers, employed in schools in the black community, came to the test site immediately after the regular school day ended on test days and were paid to administer both the achievement tests and the questionnaires to the children. Testers included both black and white teachers.

NOTES

1. James Coleman, et al., Equality of Educational Opportunity (Washington, D.C.: U.S. Government Printing Office, 1966), pp. 302-312.
2. Irwin Katz, "Some Motivational Determinants of Racial Differences in Intellectual Achievement," International Journal of Psychology, 1967, 2, pp. 1-12.
3. Alan Wilson, "Residential Segregation of Social Classes and Aspiration of High School Boys," American Sociological Review, 1959, 24, pp. 836-845.
4. Ibid.
5. V. C. Crandall, W. Katkovsky, and V. J. Crandall, "Children's Beliefs in Their Own Control of Reinforcements in Intellectual-Academic Achievement Situations," Child Development, 1965, pp. 92-109.
6. Katz, op. cit.
7. Coleman, et al., op. cit., p. 319.
8. Ibid., p. 321.
9. Ibid., p. 321.
10. Ibid., p. 324.
11. See James E. Teele, Ellen Jackson, and Clara Mayo, Family Experiences in Operation Exodus: The Bussing of Negro Children, Community Mental Health Journal Monograph No. 3 (New York: Columbia University Pres, 1967).
12. Katz, op. cit.
13. Ibid., p. 15.
14. Teele, et al., op. cit.

15. J. Rotter, M. Seeman, and S. Liverant, "Internal versus External Control of Reinforcements: A Major Variable in Behavior Theory," in N. F. Washburn (ed.), Decisions, Values, and Groups (London: Pergamon Press, 1962), II.

16. J. S. Coleman, E. Q. Campbell, C. Hobson, J. McPartland, A. Mood, F. Weinfield, and R. York, Equality of Educational Opportunity (Washington: Office of Education, U.S. Department of Health, Education and Welfare, 1966).

17. L. Srole, "Social Integration and Certain Correlaries," American Sociological Review, December 1956, pp. 709-16.

18. L. Srole, op. cit.

19. V. J. Crandall, W. Katkovsky, and A. Preston, "Conceptual Formulation for Some Research on Children's Achievement Development," Child Development, XXXI (1960), pp. 787-97.

20. B. Rosen and R. C. D'Andrade, "The Psychological Origins of Achievement Motivation," Sociometry, XXII (1959), pp. 185-218.

4

PROBLEMS
IN IMPLEMENTATION

The problems I encountered in attempting to carry out the evaluative research design presented in the previous chapter were numerous. They included the failure of new parents to register early, miscalculations of projected estimates of new enrollees for September 1967, lack of adequate cooperation from the educational bureaucracy, and a variety of problems stemming from the politics of school integration. These problems will be dealt with under the headings of Obtaining New Exodus Enrollees, Obtaining a Control Group, and Program Dropouts.

PROBLEMS IN OBTAINING
NEW EXODUS ENROLLEES

The research design had included an estimate of 100 new families including about 250 children in grades 3 through 6. Actually the Exodus staff had felt that as many as 400 new children in grades 3-6 from 200 families might be enrolled in Exodus by August, but I had chosen to be conservative, since the previous year's experience (1966-67) had indicated that the staff was not able to predict accurately the number of children who would enroll. Also the staff, for various reasons, had shown a tendency to exaggerate the number of children in Exodus. So I had assumed that an estimate of 100 new families and 250 new children in grades 3-6 was a conservative one. I had assumed also in the research proposal that the new mothers (mothers were the preferred respondents) would be enrolled by the middle of August 1967. This assumption was based on the promises and predictions of the program staff, and indeed the staff had made an earnest effort to get those interested in the program to come into the office and register early, in July and August.

A check with the staff at the beginning of August showed that only a few new families had enrolled in the program. Another check during the middle of August revealed that fewer than 15 new families had registered for the coming school year. Thus the staff was forced to conclude that we could not know how many new parents would be enrolled in the program until school-opening day, the second week of September. This also meant, of course, that we would not know who these parents were—their names, addresses, and their children's prior schools—until the beginning of school. The effect of this was to throw off my entire timetable: interviewing of Exodus parents could not begin in August, the names of the newly enrolled Exodus children could not be sent to the superintendent's office, and I was faced with the prospect of having to attempt to undertake simultaneously not only the interviewing of Exodus and non-Exodus parents but the testing of Exodus and non-Exodus children in September and early October—if indeed the study was to commence at all.

What happened? Why did the Exodus staff miscalculate in their projection of early registrations? In addition to the obvious reason that anyone can make a mistake, it should be emphasized that anyone who is relatively new to school administration problems (such as guessing the number of new registrants for a program) will make mistakes. But this was a miscalculation of such proportions that my research plans, which had allowed for some error and were conservative, were also thrown off. Why had both the parent group and the researcher miscalculated? One of the important reasons for our mistake stemmed from the Boston educational bureaucracy.

In the past Operation Exodus had never had much cooperation from the Boston School Board. During the first year of the busing operation various members of the Boston School Committee, and especially Mrs. Louise Hicks, the chairman, invariably sniped at the program, deriding its organizers for "taking little children away from their own neighborhood" and for attempting to "destroy the neighborhood schools." The school superintendent, in tune with the School Committee, had also failed to recognize or even to discuss educational issues and problems with the parents in Exodus. However, in the early part of the second year of the program the superintendent began to refer more favorably to Operation Exodus. Although they failed to contribute one cent to the expenses incurred by Operation Exodus, the educational bureaucracy, with the superintendent as spokesman, began to speak of Exodus as if it were a program conceived and designed by the Boston school authorities in an attempt to comply with laws against racial segregation in schools. Thus, in Boston in October 1966, at the hearings held by the United States Commission on Civil Rights for the purpose of studying racial isolation in schools, the Boston school superintendent stated:

If any group can testify to the effectiveness of Boston's Open Enrollment Policy, that group is the sponsors of Operation Exodus. This program to enroll children from predominantly non-white schools into predominantly white schools was initiated and has been operated and financed through the efforts of private individuals and community groups in the Roxbury-North Dorchester areas. <u>It owes its smooth and effective implementation, in no small part, to the open seat count supplied by the Boston Public Schools.</u>[1] (Emphasis added.)

It was no small feat for the superintendent to claim to be helping Operation Exodus when he had previously never had a kind word for the program. However, since it was to the school administration's credit to boast about the Exodus program, it should not be surprising that he was now claiming credit for giving assistance at the same time that he admitted Exodus was privately financed.

Still, this statement was a recognition of the program's contribution to the goal of school racial balance. Moreover, in a letter to President Nathan M. Pusey of Harvard, dated October 18, 1966, the superintendent had come out in favor of evaluative research on Exodus. In view of his new position on this matter, it was believed that the school department would be cooperative about providing information on available school seats for the 1967-68 school year. This optimism was not justified.

The superintendent's office had promised to provide the Exodus staff with the number and location of vacant seats available in schools outside the black community by early July 1967. This information was not made available in July; neither was it available in early August. It was the latter part of August before the Exodus staff received any information at all concerning the number and location of vacant seats. The Boston school system had several additional ways of blocking the Exodus program and "open enrollment." These included the dispensation of misinformation on the location of vacant seats, the violation of the "first come, first serve" principle by preferential treatment of certain (white) students, and the requiring of personal interviews, which are not otherwise required by the school department or School Committee. These interviews were used to determine the race of applicants for transfer and to discourage applicants who were not desired by the receiving school.*

---

*Years later, in 1971, the Massachusetts Commission Against Discrimination officially took note of these practices and ruled that the administration of Boston's open enrollment program discriminated against black students (<u>Boston Globe</u>, March 20, 1971).

It is interesting that many of these same blocking tactics with respect to school integration attempts via open enrollment had been successfully practiced by school officials in New York City between 1961 and 1965.[2]

In view of the lack of adequate and early information concerning seat availability, it is not surprising that the Exodus staff was unable to provide interested black parents with the information they needed, and that consequently the parents could not enroll early. What was surprising was that in spite of an openly avowed claim to administering an effective open enrollment program and a promise to cooperate fully with Operation Exodus, the superintendent's office failed to work more closely and effectively with Operation Exodus, a program that did not cost it a dime.* It is only hindsight that suggests the expectations of the Exodus staff and of the researcher were naive.

Not only was there almost a complete lack of early registration of new Exodus enrollees for the 1967-68 school year, but the number of new enrollees in the program fell far short of the goal. When registration finally did take place, in early September, a disappointingly small number of new parents and children enrolled in the program. Instead of 100 new families there were only 75, and instead of 250 new Exodus children in grades 3-6 there were only 95 even when grades 7 and 8 were added. Thus a quick decision was made to include children attending grades 7 and 8 in the study. There is little doubt that these lower-than-expected figures were due in no small part to the tactics and practices of school officials in the administration of the open enrollment program. The low registration may also have been due in part to confusion among the Exodus staff engendered by the rush of last-minute information and changing information concerning seat vacancies, the growth of METCO, a program for the busing of Roxbury children to suburban schools (this point was discussed earlier in the background chapter), and a growing vocalization in the black community against school integration and in favor of improving and developing black schools (public and private) in the black community. It is this latter consideration that the author believes to be the most important of the three and that will be expanded here.

In previous years (1965 and 1966) it was obvious to anyone who took the time to notice that the school bureaucracy in Boston did not make a serious effort to change the way the schools were administered,[3] nor did the school board seem to be concerned with furthering

---

*It is entirely possible, of course, that this failure on the part of school officials might not have been entirely due to hostility toward school integration; it might well have been due, in part, to administrative incompetence.

46

school integration, which had been mandated by the state legislature in 1965. During these years there had been much conflict and hostility expressed publicly between the school officials and members of the black community, including staff members of Operation Exodus. By early 1967 many persons in the black community had begun to believe that the school officials had convincingly demonstrated a timeless opposition to the provision of educational opportunities for black children. Some black parents despaired of trying to educate their children anywhere in Boston's public schools and began to develop a black private school system. In this way members of the black community—including some of the staff of Operation Exodus—began to formulate a program that would give local black parents a voice in the way schools in the black community were operated.* While several black-run private elementary schools were operating by 1967, it had been believed that their small enrollment plus the fact that many black parents could not afford to pay the tuition required would still leave many black parents whose only hope for a quality education for their children was to transport them to predominantly white schools under open enrollment. This assumption may have been ill-founded. Instead, it is believed that the continued opposition (whether visible or felt) by school officials and many white parents toward school integration in Boston, along with the development of a movement toward community participation in and/or control of the administration of schools attended by black children, did much to dampen the desire of black parents to enroll their children in the Exodus program.

Thus it is the author's belief that a number of factors contributed to the fact that far fewer than the expected number of new children

---

*Thus by 1967 three privately supported black elementary public schools were operating in Roxbury: The New School, The Community School, and The Highland Park Free School. Moreover, by 1968 black parents had secured some voice (however limited) in the operation of two junior high schools in the community. The fact that some of the Exodus staff were also involved in the development of community schools may seem paradoxical at first glance, but it is not surprising if it is realized that Exodus was a leading educational organization in the black community and attempted to serve the educational needs of parents outside as well as in the busing program. For a more extended discussion of the issue of control of schools see James Teele and Clara Mayo, "School Racial Integration: Tumult and Shame," Journal of Social Issues, January 1969, and James Teele, "Black Family, Voluntary Association and Education Bureaucracy," paper presented at the meetings of the American Sociological Association, San Francisco, 1969.

were enrolled for the 1967-68 school year. In sum, it is believed that the three primary factors involved were the lack of energetic and sincere efforts to aid Exodus by the Boston School Department in its administration of the open enrollment program, the growth of METCO, and a continuing charged atmosphere due to the educational conflicts in Boston, conflicts that let to a movement by blacks to develop a community-controlled and responsive school system in the black community.

PROBLEMS IN OBTAINING A CONTROL GROUP

Many of the same factors that were operating to inhibit both the early enrollment of new Exodus families and the number of such enrollment appeared to operate with varying degrees of effect to inhibit the securing of a control group of non-Exodus parents and children. The most important of these factors were the amount of effective cooperation received from school officials and the political atmosphere surrounding the issue of school integration. In addition, the very fact that registration of new Exodus enrollees took place so late (mostly in September) automatically served to postpone both the securing and the testing of the control group. The two factors indicated above, however, operated strongly to delay formation of and weaken the control group. Thus the group of non-Exodus families was not secured until late November (and it is not claimed that they con- stituted a time control group, although the term "true control group" is used for the sake of brevity and contrast), and achievement tests and questionnaires could not be administered to the large majority of non-Exodus children until December—some three months after these data were obtained from the Exodus children. Moreover, I was able to obtain only a fraction of the desired number of non-Exodus children. These problems necessitated a change in my strategy of data analysis, as we shall see in Chapter 5. For the moment, however, I shall briefly elaborate on the two problems mentioned above.

PROBLEMS WITH SCHOOL OFFICIALS

The reader will recall from Chapter 3 that the school super- intendent's office (more specifically, the associate superintendent's office) had promised to cooperate with the researcher in efforts to secure a control group.* As soon as the new Exodus children were

---

*It should be noted that earlier attempts in 1965 and 1966 to obtain cooperation from the school superintendent in the research

enrolled; a list showing name, previous school attended, and prior grade was to be compiled and submitted to the associate superintendent, who was then supposed to supply the names and addresses of the two children adjacent on an alphabetized classroom list to each Exodus child at the sending school. It would then be up to the investigator to contact a parent of each adjacent child, determine the child's school status, and attempt to enlist the participation of parent and child in the study. It would be necessary to obtain cooperation from only one of the two adjacent children in order to obtain a control group of the same size as the Exodus group.

A list containing the names and other relevant information on the 95 children newly enrolled in Exodus was duly compiled in mid-September 1967 and forwarded to the associate superintendent of schools. The dispatch of the list was followed up a few days later with a telephone call to the associate superintendent. It was most important to ascertain whether the list had arrived and to urge that action be taken on it immediately, since the investigator was already running behind schedule. The associate superintendent sounded most congenial and assured me that he had already set his assistants to work on the list of adjacent children. He indicated that it should take about three weeks for the task to be completed. I expressed some concern and surprise that it would take so long, and the associate superintendent proceeded to explain the nature of the problem. He would have to send the name of each of the Exodus children to the child's principal at the sending school, and the principal would then have to consult his classroom lists. The associate superintendent also reminded me that there were 39 sending schools involved, including both elementary and junior high schools.

I was somewhat dismayed to learn that the task of obtaining my control group would have to be so complicated and involve so many school officials. I had not been prepared for so much bureaucratic red tape; I had assumed that copies of class lists would already be available in the office of the School Department. At the very least I had thought that the associate superintendent would simply request the relevant classroom lists from the principals involved and then have an assistant compile the data and forward them to me. However, in view of the fact that the school department was cooperating in my research for the first time after earlier refusals, I thought it discreet not to question the procedure. I was dependent on the School

---

efforts had met with failure. This lack of cooperation meant, of course, that research on the teachers could not be undertaken during the crucial early years of the project. I shall return to this problem later.

Department and did not wish to risk losing their cooperation at this time. We ended our conversation with the associate superintendent indicating that he thought I would receive my list of 190 non-Exodus children by the beginning of the second week in October. I estimated that I could have all my interviewers in the field immediately upon receiving the information and obtain the non-Exodus parents' consent by the end of the third week in October. Then I would test and administer questionnaires to the control group of non-Exodus children during the last week of October, or only one month after the completion of data-gathering on the Exodus children. As we shall see, I was dreaming.

During the first week in October I did hear from the associate superintendent of schools by mail. He enclosed a couple of notes from school principals. One principal, from a junior high school, wanted to know if he should use the list of students from the home-room or the English class. Another indicated that his lists were stratified by IQ level and alphabetized within IQ ranges. I called the associate superintendent and told him that he should have the principal in the junior high school use the homeroom list and that he should direct the second questioner to alphabetize his classroom list without regard for IQ level. The associate superintendent said that he would convey my instructions to the principals concerned.

Other principals also raised questions during the following weeks, often in time-consuming letters sent to the associate superintendent, who then relayed their questions to me.* One principal wanted to know if I wished the adjacent children to be the nearest child of the same sex. Another wanted to know if it mattered that the adjacent child was white. These questions were duly answered (sex did not matter, and race was not to be considered by the principals since there were so few white children in the sending schools). In the second week of October the information began to trickle in from some of the school principals. Since I wished to test the children in groups, both for convenience and because that was the way the new Exodus children had been tested, I had decided not to collect data from the children until all of the 39 schools involved had been heard from. In the meantime, however, as soon as the information came in from a sending school, interviewers were sent out to attempt to interview the mothers concerned and to request that their children be allowed to participate in the study.

---

*Earlier I had offered to station my research assistant in the office of the associate superintendent in order to expedite these matters, but the associate superintendent had not thought this necessary

It was not until mid-November that all of the 39 schools had been heard from, with the majority of the principals' information arriving during the second week of November. Moreover, the information was patchy and below expectations. A number of the principals stated that the list of Exodus children included names of some children who had not attended their school. (The names of all sending schools for new Exodus children had been obtained from the children's mothers and it was unlikely they were in error. A further check with the superintendent's office revealed that there had been some turnover of principals and teachers in some of these schools, which led to some difficulty in trying to locate "missing" children. In such cases adjacent non-Exodus children were never obtained.) Other principals sent information on only one adjacent child, which reduced the possibility of obtaining a comparison non-Exodus child for the Exodus child involved. Thus, instead of receiving the names of 190 adjacent non-Exodus children, the investigator received the requested data on 80 non-Exodus children. (It should be noted here that tests and questionnaires had been administered to 80 of the 95 newly enrolled Exodus children in September. In the remaining 15 cases either the child's parent had objected to the child's inclusion in the study or the child was absent from school on test dates.)

Although it might seem that the 80 non-Exodus children, provided all the parents agreed to participate in the study, would have represented an adequate control group, such was not the case. In at least 20 instances there was no adjacent child for an Exodus child, and in a like number of cases there were names of two adjacent non-Exodus children. Thus even if all the parents of the non-Exodus children had consented to their children's participation in the study, the investigator would still have comparison cases for only 60 of the new Exodus children. Although the investigator would have liked to continue the search for comparison cases for the 20 Exodus children without a "match," the pressure of time precluded such an attempt. It was decided that the research team's time would be best spent in attempting to persuade all the parents of the adjacent non-Exodus children to participate in the study.

Consequently, while some of the non-Exodus children, whose parents had granted permission, were administered tests and questionnaires beginning in mid-November, the testing of the majority of these children had to wait until their parents were contacted and interviewed, after the middle of November. It was at this point, I believe, that the effects on members of the black community of the political atmosphere in regard to school racial integration, including the hostility of many whites to busing, began to manifest themselves.

THE POLITICAL ATMOSPHERE AND
THE CONTROL GROUP

Some of the actions characterizing the varying attitudes toward the issue of education for black children were described in Chapter 1. These were presented as background events, i.e., they preceded the initiation of Operation Exodus in 1965.[4] However, the conflict that existed between many black parents and the Boston school administration did not end with the formation of Exodus. Although the parents in Exodus picked up support from many individual whites as well as from the State Board of Education the local school bureaucracy and the school committeemen—and committeewoman—continued to play adversary roles. The local newspapers in 1965, 1966, and 1967 were full of evidence of this. There was no shortage of innuendo and insult by school officials concerning the education and educability of black children. Most of these voices were raised with respect to the city's plan for compliance with the state law against school racial imbalance, which had been passed in the summer of 1965. The School Committee's plan, offered in early 1966, was a vague one based on open enrollment and the feeble expansion of a poor compensatory education program. The State Board of Education had not liked the School Committee's plan to end racial imbalance and had ordered it to file an acceptable plan, or state education funds for Boston would be jeopardized. Indeed, the State Board itself had sponsored various plans, which were rejected by the Boston School Committee. The State Board had not expected that all of the 46 imbalanced schools in Boston would be racially integrated by September 1966; it simply wanted the Boston Education Department to show good intentions in the form of a workable plan that would steadily reduce the number of racially imbalanced schools.

After the details of one such state plan were leaked in April 1966 (the plan would send 2,000 of 20,000 children currently attending all-black schools to predominantly white schools and eliminate racial imbalance in 4 of the 46 imbalanced schools), the politicians on the Boston School Committee really went to work. Mrs. Louise Day Hicks, who repeatedly rode the "neighborhood school" issue into office, was quoted as stating to her constituents that the state suggestions were "made by a computer which didn't take into consideration the emotions of the citizens." She added: "You need not fear that this plan will ever go into effect, because we have the votes against it on the Committee."[5] William E. O'Connor, another member of the School Committee, also had his say on this occasion, declaring that there was no evidence "that integrated education is educationally desirable. The problem is not the teachers but the failures of the [black] parents."[6] Such was the political capital numerous school officials made of the issue of school integration.

52

Then, along about this time, spring 1966, the Meredith March took place in Mississippi and the "Black Power" movement made its appearance. Although some blacks were reluctant to embrace this slogan for fear of appearing racist, a number of blacks in the northern ghettoes were ready and eager to move in the direction now called for by a growing number of long-frustrated black leaders. Simply put, this movement called on blacks to stop aspiring to integration (including school integration), to stop hoping—for the present—for white acceptance, and to develop and control their own organizations and communities. Blacks were urged to have pride in themselves, to develop their skills, and to demand power to control their own destiny.

Also, in the summer of 1966, the well-known Coleman report appeared (see Chapter 3). This report covered a large-scale study of the factors related to scores made by black and white students in public schools on achievement tests. Coleman's main finding was that black children in more racially balanced schools typically scored higher than black children in all-black or predominantly black schools. The researchers elaborated on this relationship in various ways; for example, they noted that one reason black children achieved higher scores in racially balanced schools was the association of the factor of racial mix with social class. Coleman emphasized concurrently that school facilities and teacher components accounted for far less of the variance in scores than did school racial composition. Many responsible reviews of the Coleman report appeared.

Some of the reviewers claimed that Coleman had shown that teachers and facilities were relatively unimportant.[7] Others claimed that reanalysis of Coleman's data suggested that Coleman had underestimated the weight of the school and teacher factors.[8] Be that as it may, many blacks had long been annoyed not only with the repeated finding that blacks were not learning in school but with the persistent insinuations that this was the fault of the black children. Here was yet another study of the same sort, it was thought. Now it was being claimed that one did not need to improve teacher training, expend more money on teachers' salaries, improve black schools, modify teacher attitudes toward black children, or hire more black teachers; all one needed to do was send black children to schools with white children, and black children would learn to read and write. Not all blacks, of course, responded in this way, but it is known that a good many articulate blacks did, and this articulation contributed to and became a part of the heated debate over the education of black children in Boston.

Thus, during 1966 and 1967 a number of varying currents filled the air in Boston and may be fairly described as contributing to the politics of education. The term "politics" refers to the strategies and tactics employed by persons and groups with apparently divergent goals and interests with respect to the education of black children in Boston. "Politics" also refers to the fact that the issue of the education of black children became an arena in which many politicians pursued votes for the next election. The emphasis in the term "politics of education" was on politics rather than education as far as Boston was concerned. Indeed, the politics of education became so widespread (and underhanded) that many blacks were suspicious of any new educational plan.

It is believed that the mushrooming of scholarly and non-scholarly interest in the intellectual performance of black children compared with white children, typified by the Coleman report and its sequels, combined with the fierce political opposition to school integration in Boston to convince a number of blacks that there was but one strategy left: for blacks to work to help improve and control, if only in part, the schools in their community.

I am not certain of the degree to which the politics of education as described above operated in Boston, although I feel that these oppressive politics had a substantial and wearying impact on blacks. What I do know is that the number of applications* by parents to enroll their children in Exodus in 1967 was the lowest for any of the three years beginning with 1965. I also know that only 40 of the 80 non-Exodus parents agreed to allow their children to participate in the study. Twenty of these parents refused outright to allow their children to participate. Ten others indicated that they had "never heard" of Exodus—a rather strange and suspect claim for the mothers of school-age children, given the widespread publicity about Exodus. Another ten families were not living at the address supplied by the superintendent's office. Thus participation agreement was obtained for only 50 percent of the target group of 80 non-Exodus children. Furthermore, even this did not mean that I had obtained 40 individually adjacent children; in some cases there were two adjacent non-Exodus children for one new Exodus child. This meant that the "adjacent child" control group was at less than 50 percent effectiveness and virtually useless for purposes of comparison.

For reasons that will be presented more fully in the next chapter, the investigator still persisted in efforts to assess the effectiveness of the school integration aspect of Operation Exodus, deciding to undertake cohort analysis and to drop the experimental-control group analysis. Yet the new strategy, it must be admitted now, also embodied various weaknesses. For example, the various cohorts obviously experienced different political atmospheres at the time of initial involvement in Exodus.

---

*More than 200 parents applied in each of the first two years, while fewer than 100 made application during the third year.

What I have attempted to provide the reader with in the present chapter is an appreciation of the problems encountered in an attempt to evaluate a school integration effort. Some of the problems appeared to derive from bureaucratic sources, others from political consider- ations. These problems affected both the plan for securing an experimental group and the plan for obtaining a control group. While quantitative attributions of blame are not possible (except insofar as anticipated subjects never materialized), a number of factors have been described that, it is believed, played a role in inhibiting the progress of the designed research. These factors, very briefly, in- cluded the futile exhortations to pursue school racial balance directed at the Boston School Committee by state educational officials and black parents, the countless politically motivated and educationally useless proposals developed by the Boston School Committee, the rhetoric about the sanctity of neighborhood schools (which, in Roxbury at least, were not controlled by the neighborhood and were in dis- repair), emotions directed against the busing of school children, bureaucratic ineptness, the overemphasis on achievement scores (although the parents in Exodus certainly wanted their children to learn and to achieve), the misuse of open enrollment by school officials, and the issue of community control. These factors, it is suggested here, began to take a heavy toll in the summer of 1967 on the long- held belief of Boston black parents that their children would receive a quality education in integrated Boston schools. I believe that my claim is indexed both by a slackening of interest in applications to Operation Exodus and by the unwillingness of non-Exodus parents to participate in a research effort designed to assess the effectiveness of a school integration program.

The questions this research proposed to answer were, however, too important to allow the research to quietly fade away. Indeed, because the questions concerning the effects of segregated and inte- grated schooling are vital to both blacks and whites, an attempt was made to salvage the research and to deal with the issues raised in Chapter 3. This attempt is presented in the following chapter.

NOTES

1. Hearings Before U.S. Civil Rights Commission, Boston, 1966 (Washington, D.C.: U.S. Government Printing Office), pp. 318-319.

2. David Rogers, 110 Livingston Street (New York: Random House, 1969), pp. 17, 109, 299-301.

3. See Jonathan Kozol, Death at an Early Age (Boston: Houghton Mifflin, 1967), and Peter Schrag, Village School Downtown (Boston: Beacon Press, 1967).

4. For a detailed description of the Boston educational bureaucracy and some of the educational policies and practices preceding Exodus, see Peter Schrag, Village School Downtown (Boston: Beacon Press, 1967).

5. Schrag, op. cit., p. 126.

6. Ibid., p. 127.

7. For example, see Susan Stodolsky and Gerald Lesser, "Learning Patterns in the Disadvantaged," Harvard Educational Review, Fall 1967, p. 582.

8. E.g., Samuel Bowles, "Towards Equality of Educational Opportunity," Harvard Educational Review, XXXVIII, (Winter 1968), 89-99. For other studies of teachers see James Guthrie, et al., "A Survey of School Effectiveness Studies," in Do Teachers Make a Difference?, U.S. Government Printing Office, 1970, and Robert Rosenthal and Lenore Jacobson, Pygmalion in the Classroom, (New York: Holt, Rinehart & Winston, 1968). For an excellent recent study bearing on the issue of the relationship between teacher expectations and teacher interaction with students, see Pamela C. Rubovits and Martin L. Maehr, "Pygmalion Black and White," Journal of Personality and Social Psychology, February 1973, pp. 210-218. These authors found that teachers gave preferential treatment to gifted white students but tended to ignore and criticize black students.

5

PATCHING UP
THE DESIGN

In Chapter 4, I indicated that the variety of problems encountered in attempting to implement the research plan would be dealt with under three headings: obtaining new Exodus enrollees for the 1967-68 school year, obtaining a control group, and program dropouts. The first two of these topics, discussed in Chapter 4, amplified the problems involved in attempting to assess the effects of an experiment; indeed, the discussion centered mainly on the varied problems encountered in the first task—obtaining experimental and control groups. The third of these topics, program dropouts, is for several reasons treated in a separate chapter.

The main reason for treating the dropout issue separately stems from the decision made during the problem-beset data collection phase of 1967-68 to switch from experimental-control group analysis to cohort comparison. Because the comparative analysis of cohorts from different years assumes similarity in situational (and political) circumstances, the matter of extent and cause of dropping out—for and during different cohort years—is a crucial one. Thus it was decided to discuss the problem of program dropouts within the context of the new strategy. It is emphasized that the author has two main and related aims in this chapter: first, to clarify the analytic intent implied by the switch in strategy, and second, to continue the discussion of the problem and its consequences mentioned in Chapter 4, the nature of the political and educational atmosphere vis-à-vis busing and/or school racial integration.

Donald T. Campbell and Julian C. Stanley[1] have presented the advantages, disadvantages, and strategies of a variety of experimental and quasiexperimental designs. While the original design of the present study described in Chapter 3 approximated what may be conceived of as a quasiexperiment[2] (the pretest-posttest control group design), it nevertheless had one basic weakness that cast some doubt on its ultimate explanatory power: subjects were not randomly assigned to the control (comparison) and experimental groups. In spite of the impossibility of randomization, however, the researcher was of the opinion that the importance of the subject under study justified the attempt to evaluate the effectiveness of the Exodus operation. The scope and nature of the problems encountered in the attempt to obtain a comparison, i.e., control, group suggested, however, that it would be necessary to change the research strategy.

The design that most approximates the altered design (here called "cohort analysis") is what Campbell and Stanley call "The Recurrent Institutional Cycle Design: A 'Patched-Up' Design."[3] This design was made possible by the fact that children who had entered the Exodus program in the preceding two years (1965 and 1966) also were tested and completed questionnaires in the fall of 1967, or at the same time as data was collected on the new children entering in 1967. I collected these data on the 1965 and 1966 cohorts because it was possible, and had planned to use them in case of difficulty in securing a control group for the 1967 Exodus cohort. Although I had hoped to rely mainly on Exodus-non-Exodus comparisons, when problems arose that precluded obtaining an effective comparison group it was natural that consideration should be given to the possibility of utilizing the data on previous cohorts.

The institutional cycle design is presented by Campbell and Stanley as an approximation to experimentation. In their words, the institutional cycle (patched-up) design "illustrates a strategy for field research in which one starts out with an inadequate design and then adds specific features to control for one or another of the recurrent sources of (internal) validity." The "patched-up" design presented by Campbell and Stanley, which resembles the altered design under consideration in the present case, involves specific features of two "pre-experimental" designs: (1) the one-group pretest-posttest design and (2) the static-group comparison. When the two designs are used in combination the result is a set of complementary features that negates many of the weaknesses found when either of the "pre-experimental" designs is used alone. More specifically, these complementary features combine the various strengths of the cross-sectional and longitudinal methods. The altered form of the revised present study may be idealized as follows:

	One-Year Treatment Exposure	1967 Observation	One-Year Treatment Exposure	1968 Observation
Class A (1966)	X	0_1		
Class B (1967)		0_2	X	0_3

"The design," according to Campbell and Stanley, "is appropriate to those situations in which a given aspect of an institutional process is, on some cyclical schedule, continually being presented to a new group of respondents. Such situations include schools, indoctrination procedures, apprenticeships, etc. If in these situations one is interested in evaluating the effects of such a global and complex X as an indoctrination program, then the Recurrent Institutional Cycle Design probably offers as near an answer as is available from the designs developed thus far."[4] The situation of Operation Exodus, at least for the 1966 and 1967 cohorts, appears to fit that described by Campbell and Stanley as a situation of institutional cycle.

The advantage of this institutional cycle design, remarked on by Campbell and Stanley, and which seem to apply in the present case as well, is that it permits the control of a number of sources of invalidity. Some of these sources of invalidity are history, testing, instrumentation, selection, and mortality. In addition to neutralizing these sources of invalidity, it was also assumed that the altered design would in the present case also rule out regression effects, since the evaluative measures (academic performance and attitudes) being used were not employed in the acceptance of applicants for Exodus* (a caution indicated by Campbell and Stanley) and the O_1-O_2 observations were collected at the same time (i.e., are cross-sectional).

Should the cross-sectional comparison of O_1-O_2 result in differences, these differences would not be due to a test-retest effect nor to the effects of history intervening between O_1 and O_2. Moreover, the fact that the testing for O_1 and O_2 was all done at the same time would also rule out shifts in the nature of the measuring instrument as an explanation of any differences found. However, differences found in O_1-O_2 comparisons could be due to differences in recruitment from year to year (selection), to differences in experience (maturation), or to differences in dropping out of the program (mortality). With respect to mortality, Campbell and Stanley suggest that O_1 and O_2 (representing, e.g., the 1966 and 1967 cohorts) might differ simply because the kind of children who have dropped out of the 1966 cohort are still present in the 1967 cohort. This weakness would be avoided in the present case by simply postponing data analysis until the 1967 cohort has completed the school year and then eliminating from O_2 all respondents who dropped out after O_2 but before the end of the school year (June 1968). Since this procedure can be applied in the

---

*Indeed, all applicants were accepted (i.e., self-selected). The only criterion beyond applying was whether space was available at a grade-appropriate predominantly white school.

present case, the effects of dropping out of the program (mortality) could be ruled out as an explanation of O_1-O_2 differences.

The dropout problem recurs again, however, with more serious consequences, when the next step in the altered design is reached. This step involves the O_2-O_3 comparison, which would allow the researcher to rule out the effects of selection (as well as providing a further check on the effects of mortality) were it to provide the same type of difference as does the O_2-O_1 comparison. More specifically, in the present case where Exodus children resemble volunteers, the issue is whether different factors (community attitudes, pressures, and circumstances) are operating at different times to encourage parents to enroll their children in the program and whether these factors are responsible for any difference found in the O_1-O_2 comparison. (This, of course, is a problem that would not arise in a true experimental design where the subjects in the experimental and control groups are randomly assigned.) However, should the difference in the O_1-O_3 comparison closely resemble the one for the O_1-O_2 comparison, this would suggest that the difference is not due to selection factors. The same comparisons would not rule out the possible effects of maturation, a problem best solved through the application of a true experimental design.[5] Thus, of the seven independent internal sources of invalidity (and not considering the possible interaction of any of these sources) cited by Campbell and Stanley, six—history, testing, instrumentation, regression, selection, and mortality—could be ruled out through the "patched-up" design, were it successfully implemented.

It should be emphasized that the altered design presented in idealized form on page 58, was conceived of as a possibility only. The implementation of this altered design was, of course, heavily contingent upon the successful completion of both the cross-sectional phase—O_1-O_2—and the longitudinal (i.e., test-retest) phase of the research—the O_2-O_3 comparison. This latter phase, in turn, had to rely on retention of the 1967 cohort, which brings up the problem of program dropouts as well as any other factor that militated against successful retest.

As stated earlier, it was felt that the problem of dropouts could be solved for the O_1-O_2 comparison by waiting until the end of the year and eliminating from the O_1-O_2 comparison all children from the 1967 cohort who left the program before the end of the 1967-68 school year, the assumption being that a similar dropout problem had occurred for the previous (1966-67) cohort. In fact, the Exodus staff had kept a record of children who were known to have dropped out of the program. My own assessment of the dropout rate for the two cohort years, made via letter, telephone, and other communications, built on the Exodus staff's assessment. While it must be admitted that both the operational and the research staffs may have missed some children who dropped out of the program, the following table offers as close an approximation as we were able to make for the two cohort years (for children in grades 3-8 only*):

	1966-67 Cohort	1967-68 Cohort
Number of children at beginning of year	76	80
Number of dropouts	18	11
Number of children still in program at end of year	58	69

Thus approximately 24 percent and 14 percent of the children respectively had dropped out of the program by the end of their cohort year. It would seem that this dropout rate was of a size that would permit the O_1-O_2 comparison. Still, the number of parents who had removed their children from the program was not inconsequential.

When it became obvious to the researcher during the spring of 1968 that a substantial number of Exodus children were dropping out (being withdrawn) from the program, it was decided that some attempt should be made to document the reasons. It was felt that not only would such information be valuable in the interpretation of other data from the study, but such information would have great programmatic value for the staff of Operation Exodus, allowing them feedback from, perhaps, the less flattering outcomes of the busing operation. Indeed, in a move to encourage the dropout parents' honest declarations of their reasons for withdrawing their children from the program, these parents were given a chance to respond anonymously to brief questionnaires. Only a few of the parents chose to remain anonymous, to the surprise and elation of the researcher. Of the 29 questionnaires sent to the parents of the 1966 and 1967 dropouts in grades 3-8, 25 were completed and returned, and of these only five preferred anonymity.

A checklist of reasons was supplied with the following question:

"If any of the following were among your reasons for dropping out of Operation Exodus, please put a check mark beside it in the column on the right. You may check as many as you feel apply."

---

*For all grades (K-12) over a three-year period there were 114 dropouts out of a total of approximately 600 children ever in the program (19 percent).

The following frequency distribution was obtained in response to this question:

Children too young to be bused	3
Bus ride too long for children	2
Fighting on the Exodus bus	7
Children wanted to return to a neighborhood school	4
Prejudice of teachers in Exodus school	5
Prejudice of children in Exodus school	2
No noticeable improvement in education through busing	5

Similar results were obtained when parents were asked (prior to the structured question) their main reasons for removing their children from the program: difficulties with the bus ride (long, noisy, or meeting schedules) and problems with receiving schools or teachers were the most frequently cited. Obviously, and not surprisingly, the Exodus parents had many problems; this of course should not be allowed to obscure their success in keeping their program going in spite of the various difficulties encountered. Indeed, their dropout rate seems low when viewed in the context in which Exodus was operating.

To return to the patched-up design: it seemed during the early spring of 1968 that cross-sectional analysis of the 1966-67 and 1967-68 cohorts (0_1-0_2) would be possible. The next consideration was with the prospects of a "longitudinal" analysis of the 1967-68 cohort (0_2-0_3).

It was stated earlier that by the spring of 1968 11 members of the 1967-68 cohort of 80 children had dropped out of the program and could not be retested. As we shall see, however, the problem of retention for retest goes beyond the dropouts. There were at least two other factors that prevented retest; these were the inability of the research team to obtain permission from the parents to administer the posttest, due either to outright refusal or to our inability to locate the parents, and the dropping by Operation Exodus (unknown, at first, to the researcher) of two of the nine buses from the bus routes near the end of the school year, due to lack of funds. Thus, of the 69 Exodus children in the 1967 cohort who remained after the dropouts were removed, the following additional testing attrition took place by June 1968:

13 due to lack of parental consent to test

24 due to the discontinuance of buses in spring 1968

This additional attrition of 37 cases reduced the 1967 cohort to 32. Clearly, the loss of so many additional cases for retest seems disastrous to the possibility of conducting the 0_2-0_3 comparison. What were the reasons for this disappointment?

Reasons for refusal by parents to allow their children to be retested were not solicited by the researcher, who viewed such solicitation as an infringement of the rights of the subjects. Obviously, nothing can be said further about the families who could not be located or who were not at home when retest permission was sought. The dropping of the two buses meant that some of the older children—especially in grades 5-8—were required to take public transportation to school. Apparently through an oversight, the Exodus staff forgot to inform the researcher of this change for several weeks, and the retest phase was almost upon us when we were informed of the shift. Letters were sent and phone calls made, where possible, to parents who had granted permission for retest, informing them of the time and place of retest. Still, the number of children who did not appear for retest although parental permission had been granted was considerable. It is assumed that this was due to the inconvenience for the children of making an additional trip via public transportation. The Exodus buses were driven from school to the test site on test days and afterwards to the usual drop locations. Thus the element of free will or voluntariness in retest was present for the children who now rode public transportation but not for those who rode the Exodus buses.

What can be said of all this as far as the patched-up design is concerned? In the first place, it will be recalled that the patched-up design, if it was to be effectively implemented, minimally called for analyses of both O_1-O_2 and O_2-O_3 comparisons. As indicated, the number of dropouts for the two cohorts are within tolerance limits and the O_1-O_2 comparisons seem feasible. However, the added non-dropout test attrition of 37 cases was substantial and placed the possibility of undertaking O_2-O_3 comparisons in jeopardy.*

With respect to the O_2-O_3 comparison, which involved only the 1967 cohort, what does the test attrition signify? The answer may be sought in the reminder that the major function of this comparison is to rule out the effects of selection. It was stated earlier that should the difference in the O_2-O_3 comparison closely resemble the one for the O_1-O_2 comparison, this would suggest that the difference is not due to selection factors. In view of the further test attrition, however, it would seem that this would not only appear as an alternative explanation for any differences found in the O_2-O_3 comparison but could also interact with and cloud the role of selection factors. One possible solution to this problem, it seems, would be to ascertain if

---

*Since this additional nondropout test attrition did not occur during the 1966-67 cohort year, it seems logical to retain these 37 cases in the 1967-68 cohort for the O_1-O_2 comparison.

differences on O_2 comparisons exist between those posttested and those not posttested (O_3); if no differences exist, then it would seem legitimate to proceed with the O_2-O_3 comparison under the earlier assumptions about the function of this analysis. Such comparison would not, of course, have to include the program dropouts from the 1967 cohort, since the dropouts are to be excluded from the O_1-O_2 comparisons. However, because of the confusion induced by including the dropouts at one time but not at another, it was decided to lump all cases of test attrition, including dropouts, together in the assessment of differences in O_2 of subjects posttested and not posttested in the spring of 1968. The substance and results of this analysis are presented below.

It was decided to compare those pre- and posttested with those only pretested on the effect variables employed in the study and discussed in Chapter 3. The main effect variables of concern were achievement test scores (Metropolitan), feeling of control of environment, self-image, perception of own popularity with classmates, and number of white friends. Also, because of its demonstrated importance in the Coleman study, it was decided to compare these two groups on a situational factor: racial composition of the classroom. In the case of scales measuring feeling of control of environment (fate control) and self-image, scale items are presented separately and are not summed.

In every instance statistical tests of significance showed no difference between those tested at both times (T_1-T_2) and those pretested only (T_1). Thus the proportions of low scores on the Metropolitan Achievement Test are nearly equal among those who were posttested and those who were not (see Figure 1). A slightly greater proportion (but not significantly so) of those perceiving themselves as popular was found among those not posttested, almost exact proportions of children in each group reporting having two or more white friends, and quite similar proportions of children in grades 3 and 4 among those tested at both times and those only pretested agreed that they had some control over their environment. Among the older children (grades 5-8) the proportions agreeing with the following items tapping fate control are as follows:

	T_1-T_2		T_1 Only
1. Good luck is more important than hard work	25%	-	25%
2. Don't have a chance to be successful	43%	-	26%
3. Every time I try to get ahead, someone or something stops me	46%	-	28%

While none of these differences on fate control were statistically significant, two of the items reveal that those who were lost to the study were more likely to exhibit feelings of control over the environment than those who were posttested. Thus considerable caution will have to be exercised in interpretation of findings that involve these three items, especially inasmuch as two of the items were not used by Coleman below the ninth grade while I used them in grades 5-8. Indeed, because of these differences between those posttested and those not posttested, the fate control items will not be included in the O_2-O_3 observations.

Another attitudinal variable on which these two groups are compared applies only to the children in grades 5-8: self-image. There were three items purporting to tap self-image (taken, with some changes based on conceptualization, from the Coleman study). These items along with proportions of children agreeing are as follows:

	T_1-T_2	T_1 Only
1. If I could change I'd be different from myself	50%	23%
2. I can do many things well	56%	62%
3. I sometimes feel I just can't learn	47%	47%

As indicated earlier, none of these differences were statistically significant. However, since the first item shows a substantial difference, it seems wise to exclude the self-image items from the O_2-O_3 comparisons. Both fate control and self-image items will be considered in the O_1-O_2 comparisons, however.

Finally, with respect to the situational variable, 25 percent and 26.7 percent respectively of those posttested and those not posttested said that they attended predominantly or nearly all-black classes.

In the light of the absence of any statistically significant differences between those pre- and posttested and those not posttested in the effect measured, obtained on pretests (see especially Figure 1), it seems plausible to undertake the O_2-O_3 or longitudinal aspects of the analysis. This analysis, however, will not include the Coleman items, for reasons discussed above. It should be added, moreover, that the further patch-up work alluded to by Campbell and Stanley was not possible in the present study. The findings to be presented in the following chapter are based only on O_1-O_2 and O_2-O_3 analyses, and thus the rival hypothesis of maturation might still explain any gains shown in the O_1-O_2, O_2-O_3 analyses (e.g., in the acquisition of white friends) where it is expected that $O_2 < O_1$ and $O_2 < O_3$.* To at

---

*Maturation as a rival hypothesis may be reduced to some extent, however, in data analysis, since the study group is heterogeneous in age. See Campbell and Stanley, op. cit., pp. 59 and 60.

FIGURE 1

Test Status and Reading Achievement
Score (Stanine), 1967 Cohort

Test Status

		T1-T2 both	T1 only	Total	Percent
Stanine, T1	1-2	21.9	20.8		
		7	10	17	21.2
	3-4	40.6	52.1		
		13	25	38	47.5
	5-7	37.5	27.1		
		12	13	25	31.2
	Total	32	48	80	
	Percent	40.0	60.0		100.0

Chisquare Statistic = 1.207 with 2 degrees of freedom (not significant)

least some extent, however, it is believed that the steps taken to patch up the design should the expected differences be found rule out the rival explanations of history, testing, instrumentation, regression, selection, and mortality.

With respect to sources of external invalidity, the interaction of testing and the Exodus school integration operation cannot be considered as a rival hypothesis, since children in the 1966 cohort, the source of O_1 data, were not pretested. However, because of the voluntary and unique nature of the Exodus program and also because of the lack of comparable data on conditions and experiences of school integration programs in other communities and among other non-Exodus children in Boston, the reader is urged to take seriously the caveat against generalizing beyond the children studied here. Put differently, because various possible sources of external invalidity have not been controlled (e.g., the possible reactive effects of holding the tests in a different setting of administration by special testers rather than the regular teachers* the reader is not justified in generalizing the findings to be presented in the following chapter.

There is one final matter to consider before turning to the findings, and this concerns the now-forgotten control (non-Exodus) group. Although I discussed in Chapter 4 the variety of problems that this research began to encounter at the start of the 1967-68 academic year and subsequently discussed the decision to concentrate attention on cohort analyses, I have not discussed the fate of data collection on the non-Exodus group. What happened to this group? In short, the same data that were collected on the 1966 and 1967 Exodus cohorts were collected on the non-Exodus children; 40 non-Exodus children were pretested, and of these 18 were available for and took posttests. While patching up the design I had hoped that some good use might be made of the non-Exodus cases, e.g., their employment in the longitudinal analysis as a check on effects of maturation. However, because of the additional imperfections in these data (for example, the non-Exodus pretest data was collected several months later than those for the Exodus groups, and more-over, the non-Exodus group was so small that it could not be assumed to be representative of children from similar grades who did not join Exodus), it was decided to drop the control group from any further consideration in this study.

NOTES

1. Donald T. Campbell and Julian C. Stanley, Experimental and Quasi-Experimental Designs for Research (Chicago: Rand McNally, 1966).
2. Ibid., pp. 34-64.
3. Ibid., p. 57.
4. Ibid., p. 57.
5. Because of the limitations inherent in the present study's data collection procedures, only through data analysis techniques will it be possible to control for maturation. For a general discussion of the problem of maturation see Campbell and Stanley, op. cit.

---

*This procedure was of course designed to counter the likelihood that the Boston School Board would not wish to participate in the study to the extent of permitting its teachers and facilities to be used.

6

In this chapter the following tasks are undertaken: (1) the study groups will be described; (2) the two cohorts of children will be compared on selected scores and responses obtained from tests and questions administered in September 1967, one year after the 1966 cohort entered the Exodus busing program and at the time of entry for the 1967 cohort (the O_1-O_2 analysis); (3) before-and after comparisons will be presented for the 1967 cohort (the O_2-O_3 analysis). "Cohorts," of course, refers to child cohorts and not to parent cohorts. The data on parents was not collected in a manner suitable for use in connection with the child cohort analysis. The first interviews with the 1966 parents were undertaken in January and February, four or five months after their children entered the program, while the first interviews with 1967 parents were held in September, less than one month after their children entered Exodus. Therefore data from parent interviews will not be presented in connection with the children's data, though descriptive data from parent interviews will be presented near the end of the chapter.

It was decided first to undertake a description of the 1966 and 1967 cohorts on background variables before presenting the O_1-O_2 comparisons, in order that the reader may see the similarities and differences between the two cohorts.

BACKGROUND CHARACTERISTICS

The following background variables enter into the description of the two cohorts: sex, age, foreign language spoken in home, living in male-headed household, mother's work status, mother's education, number of children in the family, and a couple of items believed to be related to family socioeconomic status. (Father's occupation was omitted because too many cases were lacking this information.) This description will also serve as a check on possible differences in selection factors that might account for effect differences, should any differences be found later on in the O_1-O_2 analysis. All of the information on background factors as well as on effect measures comes from the children. The distribution of the background variables on the two cohorts are presented in Table 5.

It can be seen from Table 5 that the two cohorts are quite similar, at least in the admittedly limited number of background variables presented here. Similarly, analysis of the cohorts on a variety of other variables (e.g., father's education) revealed no differences. Some reservation is warranted with respect to the substantial number of cases of no information on the extent of the mother's education. However, the similarity of the two cohorts on background variables suggests that selection factors—where they were operating—operated in a similar fashion for both cohorts. Thus it seems reasonable now to undertake the cross-sectional comparison of the two cohorts (O_1-O_2).

CROSS-SECTIONAL COMPARISON

The reader will recall that this comparison is a part of our revised design, one that entails, in addition to the cross-sectional analysis, a longitudinal analysis to be presented later on. The design is called the Recurrent Institutional Cycle Design and was necessitated by the difficulty in obtaining an adequate control group. This design, referred to by Campbell and Stanley as a "patched-up" design, involves specific features of two "pre-experimental" designs: the one-group pretest-posttest design and the status-group comparison.[1] It is believed that when these two designs are used in combination the result is a set of complementary aspects that neutralizes many of the analytic problems that abound when either of the "pre-experimental" designs is used alone. The analytic intent in the present case may be idealized as follows:

	One-Year Treatment Exposure	1967 Observation	One-Year Treatment Exposure	1968 Observation
Class A (1966)	X	O_1		
Class B (1967)		O_2	X	O_3

TABLE 5

Frequency Distribution on Selected Background
Variables for Children in the 1966 and 1967 Cohorts
(N for 1966 Cohort = 58; N for 1967 Cohort = 69)*

Variables	1966 Cohort		1967 Cohort	
	N	Percent	N	Percent
1. Age				
7-8 years	10	18.2	13	19.1
9-10 years	19	34.5	26	38.2
11-14 years	26	47.3	29	42.7
2. Sex				
Males	28	50.0	34	50.0
Females	28	50.0	34	50.0
3. Father in home?				
Yes	41	78.8	46	68.7
No	11	21.2	21	31.3
4. Mother work full-time?				
Yes	26	52.0	33	53.2
No	24	48.0	29	46.8
5. Is foreign language spoken in home?				
Yes	6	11.3	9	14.1
No	47	88.7	55	85.9
6. No. children in home				
Three or fewer	22	44.0	31	47.6
Four or more	28	56.0	34	52.4
7. Education of mother				
Less than HSG	15	37.5	17	32.7
HSG or better	25	62.5	35	67.3
8. Telephone in home?				
Yes	47	90.4	61	91.0
No	5	9.6	6	9.0
9. Have automobile in family?				
Yes	34	66.7	43	67.2
No	17	33.3	21	32.8

*The N for the 1967 cohort is 69 because the 11 dropout cases
during the 1967-68 year are excluded from all analyses. Lack of
information on specific items accounts for all other instances where
N's for 1966 and 1967 cohorts do not equal 58 and 69 respectively.

In the present section I will present the results of a comparison
on selected effect variables that involves measures taken from children in the 1966 cohort after they had spent a year in the Exodus
busing program and from children in the 1967 cohort just before their
involvement in the busing operation.*

There are four effect (or experimental) variables on which the
two cohorts are compared: (1) achievement scores, (2) child's perception of classmates' liking for him, (3) measure of self-image, and
(4) measure of feeling of fate control (or control of environment).
The latter two measures were taken from the Coleman report,[2] and
for children in grades 5 through 8 each consists of three structured
items: In addition there is a single item that purports to tap feelings
of fate control for children in grades 3 and 4. The achievement test
used was the Metropolitan Achievement Test, Form A, a much-used
and standardized test. The measure of the child's perception of his
classmates' liking for him is based on the Colvin Silhouette Test,**
which has been used in other similar studies but is less well known
than the other measures and is thus presented here for the convenience
of the reader.

FIGURE 2

Colvin Silhouette Test

One   Two   Three   Four   Five   Six   Seven   Eight   Nine   Ten

Look at the drawing above. Make believe that they are
pictures of some of the children in your class. The first
child, number one on the numbers below the picture, is
the best liked boy or girl in the class. The least liked
one is number ten. I want you to decide about where you
belong in the line and put a circle around the right number. If you think you are the best liked person in your
class, put a circle around number two or three. If you

_____

*Actually, children in the 1967 cohort had been in the program
one or two weeks when these measures were taken.
**Reprinted by permission of Ralph Colvin.

are near the middle, you might circle four, five, or six.
The least liked you are, the higher the number you should
circle on the row of numbers. If you think you're near the
least liked but not quite, you circle number nine. If you
are the least liked of all the children, circle number ten.

These four experimental variables were mentioned in Chapter 3,
which presented the original research design; they were described
either as primary effect variables in my primary change hypothesis
(achievement) or as being central to the explication of any change
found. In view of the disasters that prevented the implementation of
the original design and led to an altered procedure, the original
hypotheses are not all testable as stated. The nearest thing to
holdover hypotheses that the present data will attempt to test are
taken from the first and fourth change hypotheses:

1. Participation in Operation Exodus results in higher achievement test scores;

2. The more accepting Exodus children feel their classmates
are of them, the greater the positive change in achievement.
None of the remaining hypotheses can be tested because of alterations
in the study design, the lack of an adequate control group, differences
between those posttested and those not posttested, and the small number of cases available. However, it seems appropriate to present the
results of cohort comparisons on the four variables, since they all
seem germane to the issue of the effects of school racial integration.

With respect to the attitude data in particular, findings must be
cautiously presented because of the problems mentioned above and
also because in some cases test-retest reliability was unsatisfactory.
Since I have not dealt previously with the issue of reliability, a brief
discussion of it is presented before proceeding to the cross-sectional
comparisons.

RELIABILITY

Although test-retest reliabilities are presented in this section,
it is emphasized that they are based on the pretest-posttest data and
thus were given eight to nine months apart. (I did not undertake a
short-range test-retest reliability check because of the danger that
memory and practice effects would inflate the extent of change between
pre- and posttest; moreover, I did not want to alienate the parents
and children through repetitive testing.) Because of this rather
lengthy time gap it can be argued that some shift between pretest and
posttest may be due to real changes having taken place; such change
may result in lower reliabilities, especially in cases where there are

only two or three response categories, as in the two Coleman attitudes: self-image and fate control. It is again emphasized that the two Coleman attitudes will be presented only in the cohort (cross-sectional) analysis and not in the change (longitudinal) analysis; this decision was dictated by the rather substantial pretest differences among members of the 1967 cohort on the Coleman attitude items between those who remained in the study and those who dropped out before posttesting (see Chapter 5).

The test-retest reliability coefficients were obtained for the Metropolitan Achievement Test, different forms of which were employed for the test and retest; the Colvin Silhouette Test, and the six items tapping the two Coleman attitudes: The first two tests were administered to children in grades 3-8 while the Coleman items were administered only to children in grades 5-8. Considering only the children in the 1967 cohort who were pre- and posttested, there were 17 children in grades 5-8 and 15 in grades 3 and 4. The test-retest reliabilities were as follows:

Metropolitan Achievement Test		.62 (N=30)
Colvin Silhouette Test		-.24 (N=11)
Fate control item 1:	"People like me don't have much chance to be successful in life."	.21 (N=15)
Fate control item 2:	"Good luck is more important than hard work for success."	.44 (N=15)
Fate control item 3:	"Every time I try to get ahead, something or somebody stops me."	.75 (N=14)
Self-image item 1:	"I sometimes feel I just can't learn."	-.10 (N=9)
Self-image item 2:	"If I could change, I'd be someone different from myself."	.04 (N=9)
Self-image item 3:	"I can do many things well."	-.29 (N=9)

Both the Colvin Silhouette Test and the Coleman self-image items appear to be unreliable as far as the present study is concerned. It is of more than passing interest that a sizable number of children did not respond to the items on perception of classmates' liking and self-image on either the pre- or posttest, this being most often the case on posttest. In contrast, nearly all of the children (grades 3-8) completed the achievement test on both test occasions and nearly all of the eligible children (grades 5-8 only) completed the fate control items on both the pre- and posttest. It could be that the children felt somewhat threatened by the self-centered items. It is likely that the lack of reliability of both the self-image items and the Colvin Test is due to the combined efforts of attitude change, the small N's employed, the small number of response categories, and measurement error. It is advisable therefore that great caution be taken in the consideration of findings to be presented for these variables. Such findings as are presented are offered only in a suggestive way. It would seem that considerably more confidence may be placed in the findings on the reading achievement test and the measure of fate control.

The problem of reliability is an important one, and the discussion here clearly shows that more attention should have been given to it earlier in the present study. Future researchers in this area would be well advised to use measures with established reliability (as was done here for the achievement test) or to establish the reliability of their measures during a pretest phase.

The cross-sectional or cohort analysis is now presented below. It is emphasized that where measures are of known unreliability it is hoped that the reader will observe necessary caution in the interpretation of results.

ACHIEVEMENT SCORES

Results of the September 1967 administration of the Metropolitan Reading Achievement Test are presented in Table 6. As expected, the children in the 1966 cohort scored somewhat higher in reading achievement than did those in the 1967 cohort. Although it is noted that the test of significance results in a $P<10$, I would argue that in studies of this type a P level of less than 10 is meaningful. With respect to reading 46 percent of the children who were just beginning to attend racially integrated schools (1967 cohort) placed in the low stanines ("2" and "3"), while only 27 percent of the one-year veterans (1966 cohort) reflected poor reading ability. Similar results obtain on the word-knowledge portion of the test: 35 percent of the 1967 cohort as opposed to only 17 percent of the 1966 cohort placed in the two low positions ("2" and "3"). It would seem that the hypothesis that the

TABLE 6

Results of Metropolitan Achievement Test
(Reading) in September 1967, Grades 3-8

| | 0_1 | | 0_2 | |
Stanines	1966 N	Cohort Percent	1967 N	Cohort Percent
Low 2	6	10.3	13	18.8
3	10	17.2	19	27.6
4	23	39.7	15	21.7
5	11	19.0	16	23.2
6	8	13.8	4	5.8
High 7	—	—	2	2.9
Total	58	100.0	69	100.0
	$\overline{X}$ =	4.1	$\overline{X}$ =	3.8

t = 1.39, .05 <P < .10, one-Tailed Test, d.f. = 125

Exodus busing program produced positive reading results for the
children involved is tenable; however, the hypothesis is subject to the
rival interpretation of selection unless the longitudinal analysis
(0_2-0_3) results in similar differences.* That is to say, perhaps some
undetected factor entered into the educational situation and caused
differences in the kinds of child represented in the two cohorts, differences that might account for the findings presented in Table 6.
However, if the same or similar magnitudes of difference exist in the
0_2-0_3 comparison as in the 0_1-0_2 comparison above, this would argue
against the selection hypothesis. These 0_2-0_3 comparisons will be
undertaken farther along in this chapter.

CHILD'S PERCEPTION OF CLASSMATES'
LIKING FOR HIM

The results of the 1967 administration of the Colvin Silhouette
Test are presented in Table 7. It is clear from Table 7 that more

*The logic of the cross-sectional analysis, however, rules out
the rival hypotheses of testing, history, instrumentation, and regression (see Chapter 5).

than twice as many children (proportionately) in the 1966 cohort compared to the 1967 cohort feel that their classmates think highly of them (rated themselves as "1" "2," or "3"). Attention to the number and proportion of "don't know" and "least liked" responses, however, leads away from the corollary notion that the new children are more likely to feel unpopular than the veterans, as such is not the case. A rather small number of children in each cohort placed themselves at the unliked end of the scale, while twice as many, proportionately, of the 1967 cohort compared to the 1966 group indicated that they did not know what their classmates thought of them. When it is realized that this picture test was administered just two or three weeks after the 1967 cohort entered a new classroom, in a new school and in a rather different environment, then it seems quite natural and logical for more of the children in the 1967 cohort to feel unable to judge their classmates' opinion of them. Being able to rate your classmates' liking for you obviously depends to some extent on how well you think they know you. Over-all, the findings suggest that, ceteris paribus, the longer a black child remains in a racially integrated class the more accepting he feels his classmates are of him. This finding, if it stands up, is important, because McPartland in his reanalysis of the Coleman

TABLE 7

Child's Perception of Classmates' Liking
for Him (Colvin Silhouette Test) in
September 1967, Grades 3-8

		O_1		O_2	
		1966	Cohort	1967	Cohort
Perception Rating		N	Percent	N	Percent
Best-liked	1	11	19.0	10	14.5
	2	12	20.7	3	4.3
	3	6	10.3	3	4.3
	4	2	3.4	8	11.6
	5	10	17.3	8	11.6
	6	2	3.4	4	5.8
	7	1	1.7	2	2.9
	8	2	3.4	2	2.9
	9	1	1.7	2	8.8
Least-liked	10	3	5.2	6	8.8
Don't know		8	13.9	21	30.4
Total		58	100.0	69	100.0

data has found that black children who attended schools characterized by cross-racial acceptance scored higher on achievement than black children who attended schools characterized by cross-racial rejection.[3] Thus the development of feelings of being accepted may be a prelude to improved academic interest and performance. The uncertainty about their reception by white students may have been one of the more difficult aspects of the school integration program for black children and may have had consequences in academic performance. After all of the basic cohort findings have been presented I shall return to this issue.

SELF-IMAGE

The third effect variable on which the cohorts are compared is self-image. Three structured items were employed in the assessment of self-image, and responses to these items were assessed separately for each item in view of some controversies about whether the items all tap self-image. These self-image items, borrowed from Coleman's study, are used in addition to the Colvin Silhouette Test of self-perception because they do not seem to be as dependent on being acquainted with one's classmates as is, to some extent at least, the Colvin Test. These data were collected only on children in grades 5-8 because it was thought inadvisable to query the very young further about their self-concept.

While the self-concept items I chose to use came from Coleman's study, they are not the same as the ones he stressed in his analysis. The ones he used were (1) "I sometimes feel I just can't learn," (2) "How bright do you think you are compared to other students in class?" and (3) "I'd do better if teachers didn't go so fast." The investigator's examination of the Coleman survey questions revealed two additional items that appeared on the surface to be better measures of self-concept than items (2) and (3). These were "If I could change, I'd be someone different from myself," and "I can do many things well." It was decided to use these latter two items along with "I sometimes feel I just can't learn" as measures of self-concept. These three items are highly interrelated, with correlation coefficients ranging from .60 to .73 for the 1967 cohort and from .63 to .83 for the 1966 cohort.

The data show that on the first two items, which are negative statements, "I sometimes feel I just can't learn" and "If I could change, I'd be someone different from myself," children in the 1966 cohort were more likely to reject statements reflecting a negative self-concept. This tendency was stronger on the second item, where 19 percent and 31 percent respectively of the 1966 and 1967 cohorts agreed.

However, on the third item, "I can do many things well," which is positively stated, children in the 1967 cohort were more likely to render the preferred response; 62 percent of the 1967 cohort and 55 percent of the 1966 cohort agreed with the statement. While one wonders if the differences are a result of yeasaying and naysaying, it seems that the most reasonable conclusion is that no clear differences between groups emerge from these items. The findings on these items suggest that better measures of self-image are needed and that researchers should be as concerned about the acquisition of a positive self-concept as they are about achievement scores among black children involved in school racial integration programs, especially since Coleman found that self-concept was strongly and directly related to scores on achievement tests, also a matter that will be considered later in this chapter.

FATE CONTROL

Another set of three items from the Coleman study, tapping fate control, comprises the fourth and last of the effect variables to be presented here.

The three items used, which were employed by Coleman, were (1) "People like me don't have much of a chance to be successful in life," (2) "Good luck is more important than hard work for success," and (3) "Every time I try to get ahead, something or somebody stops me." For both cohorts the three items were strongly intercorrelated, supporting the notion that they were tapping the same dimension. The coefficients ranged between .81 and .84 for the 1967 cohort and .68 and .72 for the 1966 cohort. Coleman and his colleagues found that children's feelings about their ability to make the environment respond to their efforts (fate control) were quite strongly related to achievement test scores—indeed, more strongly related than any of the other attitudes included in their study. It was expected that the comparison of the two cohorts, grades 5-8 only, would reveal that a year in the Exodus program had a measurable and positive effect on the children's feelings of fate control.

As with the self-image items, in two of the three fate-control items, "People like me don't have much chance to be successful" and "Every time I try to get ahead, something or somebody stops me," the 1967 cohort had a smaller proportion of respondents giving the "preferred" response, indicating they feel they can make the environment respond to their efforts: 27 percent of the 1967 cohort and 16 percent of the 1966 cohort agreed with the first statement while 39 percent of the former and 32 percent of the latter cohort agreed with the second statement. On the remaining item, "good luck is more important than hard work for success," the 1967 cohort had a higher proportion of respondents who gave the response that indicates a feeling of control over the environment, with 22 percent of the 1967 cohort and 39 percent of the 1966 cohort agreeing with the statement. Thus on the fate control items, too, no clear difference emerges between the two cohorts. Furthermore, nay- or yeasaying cannot account for the fact that children in grades 5-8 in the 1967 cohort gave more desirable responses on the "good luck" item than their counterparts in the 1966 cohort, since all three items are negatively phrased.

With respect to the younger children (grades 3 and 4) it was felt permissible to phrase one question purporting to assess their feelings about fate control: "Do you think you'll be able to be what you want to be when you grow up?" While children in the 1966 cohort, as expected, were more likely to respond affirmatively to this question, the difference (90 percent vs. 77 percent) was not a very striking one.

In sum, then, no substantial differences emerge between the two cohorts on the Coleman items tapping self-concept and feelings of fate control, although there is a hint of slightly favorable changes having taken place in the 1966 cohort. It now remains to be seen whether the Coleman items, the responses to the Colvin Silhouette Test, a set of situational variables, and subject characteristics show any relationship to achievement scores.

EXPLICATION OF ACHIEVEMENT SCORES

The clearest differences between the two cohorts appeared on the first two effect variables: achievement scores and perception of being liked by classmates. These differences, in view of design strategy, are attributable to the effects of busing, at least until the 02-03 comparisons rule otherwise. The purpose of the present examination of relationships between achievement scores and other variables is to permit possible inferences to be made about a limited range of more specific factors relating to achievement test outcome. That is, I am looking for clues that might suggest why children in either group perform the way they do as well as for clues that might help explain the differences between cohorts.

The first relationship to be examined is the relationship between the child's perception of extent of being liked by classmates and his achievement scores (reading test). McPartland has indicated in a re-analysis of Coleman's data that black children who attended schools characterized by cross-racial acceptance scored higher on achievement tests than children who attended schools characterized by cross-racial rejection. In the present case I wish to ascertain if the Exodus children in each of the two cohorts who feel well liked are also more likely to score higher on the achievement test than children who do not feel well liked or who do not know how their classmates feel about them. These cross-tabulations are presented in Table 8.

The relationships shown in Table 8 merit the careful attention of the reader. Among the children who feel well liked by their classmates a majority score below the fifth stanine in each cohort. However, whereas 41 percent of those who feel best liked in the 1966 cohort place in the fifth or a higher stanine, only 31 percent of those who perceive themselves as best liked are in the fifth, sixth, or seventh stanine in the 1967 cohort. Indeed, if the relationships for each cohort are reconstructed, the following fourfold tables appear for the two cohorts:

	1966 Cohort		1967 Cohort	
	Stanines 2-4	Stanines 5-7	Stanines 2-4	Stanines 5-7
Best or fairly well-liked	26	17	25	11
Least liked or don't know	13	3	22	11

$$x^2 = 6.06, 1 \text{ df}, p<.05 \qquad \text{NS}$$

Thus it is easily seen what the main differences between the two cohorts are: First, children in the 1966 cohort who perceive themselves as best or well liked are more likely than their 1967 counterparts to place in the higher reading stanines; second, children in the 1966 cohort who perceive themselves as least liked or who do not know where they stand with classmates are substantially likelier to place in the lower stanines than their counterparts in the 1967 cohort.

To recapitulate: children in the 1966 cohort scored higher in reading achievement and were also likelier to perceive themselves as being well liked by their classmates. In addition, fewer of the children in the 1966 cohort felt that they did not know how their classmates perceived them. When these two variables are cross-tabulated, a "relationship" is found to exist for the 1966 cohort but not for the 1967 cohort. What is to be made of these findings? It seems logical to assume that the factor of uncertainty is operating here: the children in the 1966 cohort have had a year's experience and they know how their classmates and teachers feel about them. Presumably they are also aware of how the school's reward system works. When children in the 1966 cohort feel unwelcomed and unwanted their academic work suffers, but when they feel accepted their academic performance

TABLE 8

Child's Perception of Classmates' Liking
for Him and Reading Achievement Score
in September 1967, Grades 3-8

1966 Cohort (N = 58)
Reading Stanine

Perception of Classmates' Liking	2-3 (low)		4		5		6-7		100
	N	Per-cent	N	Per-cent	N	Per-cent	N	Per-cent	Per-cent
1-3 (Best-liked)	8	27.6	10	34.5	7	27.1	4	13.8	29
4-6	5	35.7	3	21.4	2	14.3	4	28.6	14
7-10	1	14.3	6	85.7	—	—	—	—	7
Don't know	2	25.0	4	50.0	2	25.0	—	—	8

r = -.12 N. S.

1967 Cohort (N = 69)
Reading Stanine

Perception of Classmates' Liking	2-3		4		5		6-7		100
	N	Per-cent	N	Per-cent	N	Per-cent	N	Per-cent	Per-cent
1-3	6	37.5	5	31.2	3	18.8	2	12.5	16
4-6	11	55.0	3	15.0	4	20.0	2	10.0	20
7-10	5	41.7	3	25.0	3	25.0	1	8.3	12
Don't know	10	47.6	4	19.1	6	28.6	1	4.7	21

r = -.03 N. S.

is likely to improve also. In either case the problem of not knowing how their classmates feel about them has been resolved. The children in the 1967 cohort are in strange surroundings; they are more likely than those in the 1966 cohort either to feel that they are not very well liked or to feel uncertain about other's perceptions of them. In either case they do not do as well on the achievement test, but this performance is not related to their perception of their classmates' liking for them. It can only be assumed that McPartland's findings with Coleman's data are holding, i.e., that those black children who feel accepted score higher on achievement tests than those who feel themselves in hostile environments—the precise case with the 1966 cohort. The relationship does not hold for the 1067 cohort because their perceptions and feelings have not been confirmed by experience.

It is possible, however, that this interpretation, which treats perception of other's liking as the independent variable, could be wrong, and that good academic performance precedes being liked, and the perception of being liked, by one's peers. I can think of no argument against this rival interpretation since the data being presented were all collected at the same point in time and the relationships will support either interpretation. The preferred interpretation, of course, places substantially more importance on the "definition of the affective situation" by incoming black students, an interpretation consistent with McPartland's finding.

Katz, too, has dealt with the affective situation in his discussion of an expectancy model.[4] Katz states that "expectancy" refers to the person's "estimate of the probability that a given situation will have a favorable or unfavorable outcome for him." With regard to achievement he suggests that there are two probability estimations: one is the student's self-estimate for attaining a certain standard of performance and the other is the student's degree of confidence in the responsiveness of the social environment. Katz states that "present scales do not distinguish between the two types of expectancy that . . . [are] operative in academic achievement situations for Negroes."[5] While I did not attempt to measure what Katz calls the estimation by the student of his chances for attaining a certain standard of performance, the reader will recall that the child's feeling of fate control—or responsiveness of the social environment—was measured. The relationships (Pearsonian coefficients) between each of the items measuring the responsiveness of the environment and reading achievement test results were examined for children in each of the two cohorts.

The coefficients of correlation between these items and reading achievement were all in the expected direction, but none of the magnitudes reached statistically significant levels. The comparison showed a weaker relationship among the children who have spent a year in the Exodus program. Only with respect to "People like me don't have much chance. . . ." was the relationship stronger for the 1966 cohort: .15 vs. .09. The lack of any significant relationships is disappointing in view of the finding presented by Coleman[6] that "of all the variables measured in the survey, including all measures of family background and all school variables, these attitudes showed the strongest relation to achievement." He also found that fate control had a particularly strong relation to achievement among blacks. Perhaps the obvious conclusion is that feelings of control over the environment are not as strongly related to achievement test outcomes for blacks as Coleman had concluded from his data; however, there are several considerations that caution against rejecting Coleman's findings on the basis of the present study. First of all, of the three items utilized in the present study on children in grades 5-8, Coleman used only one on children as low as grade 6: "People like me don't have much chance to be successful," and this was the only such item Coleman used in grade 6. The other two items, along with the sixth-grade item, were employed by Coleman in the ninth and twelfth grades. Thus it is entirely possible that this fact alone would cause findings divergent from Coleman's. Secondly, Coleman found that the variance accounted for among black children increased with grade; the highest grade in Coleman's study was grade 12, and in the present study, grade 8. Finally, the small N and also the attrition in the present study group make it unwise to use present findings to challenge findings from other studies.

The relationships between each of the Coleman items purporting to tap self-concept and reading achievement were next examined for each of the two cohorts, and, as in the case of fate control, none of the self-image items reached a level of statistical significance; moreover, one of the coefficients (involving "If I could change . . ." and the 1967 cohort) was not even in the expected direction. Again, in attempting to solve the puzzle of why self-image (and at least one of the three items is the same as one of Coleman's measures of self-image) was related to achievement in the Coleman report but not in the present study, readers should keep in mind that the present N is quite small, the items are unreliable for this study group, two of the items are different from Coleman's, and there is more homogeneity (of grade, of region, and of sociocultural characteristics) in the present study group. Readers may also wish to remember that response to one of the two added items ("If I could change I'd be someone different from myself") was rather substantially related to whether a child from the 1967 cohort was posttested or not in May 1968, with test attrition cases being likelier to disagree with the item (see Chapter 5). On the other hand, there was no relationship at all between test attrition and the one self-image item common to both studies: "I sometimes feel I just can't learn." However, because I did find some differences between test attrition and items in both the fate control and self-concept measures for the 1967 cohort, and also because of the other weaknesses associated with the use of these items in this study, it was decided to drop all of the items in these two measures from the longitudinal analysis (O_2-O_3), which will be presented later on in this chapter. Thus the puzzle will be left at this point. One can only conjecture that perhaps the assumptions about what these items are measuring are wrong or that the study group employed here is atypical. Indeed, with respect to self-concept, at least, the Colvin Silhouette Test resulted in a more plausible and expected relationship to reading achievement, lending some credence to the notion that self-concept is important to achievement but that further work on it must be done with respect to black children.

The final set of cross-tabulations from the O_1-O_2 analysis of of achievement test outcomes involves the relationships between situational/individual characteristics and achievement scores. Pearsonian coefficients showing these relationships are presented in Table 9.

None of the variables listed in Table 9 are significantly related to reading achievement for either cohort. Variable 2, sex, almost attains a statistically significant level for the 1966 cohort, however, as do variables 3 (nonwhite teacher last year) and 4 (number of white friends) for the 1967 cohort. Specifically, girls placed higher than boys on achievement test results, and incoming children (1967 cohort) with white friends or who had had white teachers the previous year scored higher on achievement than cohort colleagues who had not. It is emphasized, however, that none of the five variables in Table 9 are statistically related at the .05 level to achievement test placement.

Indeed, with the exception of the Colvin Silhouette Test self-ratings when categories were combined, none of the twelve variables under analysis here was significantly related to reading achievement at the .05 level; the highest magnitude exists for "number of white friends" claimed by the child, .22. Doubtless some unmeasured situational factors or attitudinal components (such as the challenge present, the child's motivation, or teacher/school influences) or both exist that would help account for variation in achievement test scores.

The fact remains, however, that the O_1-O_2 analysis suggest two interesting effects of the Exodus program, moderate though they may be. The first is that some differences appear between the two cohorts on both parts of the Metropolitan Achievement Test, reading and word-knowledge; and the second is that a moderately strong difference appears to exist on the Colvin Silhouette Test measuring the child's perception of his classmates' liking for him. The logic of the design employed, it is believed, may allow these differences to be attributed to the busing program if supported in the O_2-O_3 analysis, although admittedly the investigator was unable to pinpoint clearly factors in the process that might have made possible a fuller explanation.

The reader may recall that it had been the early hope of the investigator to employ data from parents in the explication of findings; however, the fact that the pretest data on parents in the two cohorts were not obtained at similar points in the study argued against the use of much of the parent data in the explanatory task. Moreover, there was test attrition also among the parents: some refused permission for the child to be tested while submitting to interviews themselves, while others denied us the requested interview but permitted the child to be tested. Because of incongruent overlap between parent and child data, any attempt to employ parent data in the explanation of findings would have further reduced the size of the children's

TABLE 9

Pearsonian Coefficients Between Five Situational
and Individual Characteristics and
Achievement, September 1967

Situational-Individual Characteristics	1966 Cohort			1967 Cohort		
	r	N	Significance Level	r	N	Significance Level
1. Age	-.10	58	NS	-.02	69	NS
2. Sex	.21	56	NS	.15	69	NS
3. Nonwhite teacher last year	.09	53	NS	.20	63	$P < .10$
4. Number of white friends	.10	54	NS	.22	60	$P < .10$
5. Number of white students in your class now (grades 5-8 only)	-.04	31	NS	-.12	35	NS

study group. Consequently the pursuit of explanations of 0_1-0_2 findings cannot meaningfully be carried further. What can be pursued further, however, is the longitudinal analysis that was conducted on the 1966 cohort—an analysis referred to as the 0_2-0_3 comparison. The reasons for undertaking the 0_2-0_3 analysis were discussed in Chapter 5 and will be briefly reviewed before the presentation of findings.

LONGITUDINAL ANALYSIS OF THE 1967 COHORT

As stated in Chapter 5, the major function of the 0_2-0_3 analysis was to rule out the effects of selection. That is, should the difference in the 0_2-0_3 comparison resemble the one for the 0_1-0_2 comparison ($0_2 < 0_1$ and $0_2 < 0_3$), this would suggest that the difference is not due to selection factors. Analysis of the background factors describing each cohort has already provided us with some evidence that the two cohorts are similar. It would be reassuring as far as the selection problem goes, however, if the results of longitudinal analysis resemble those for the cross-sectional analysis on the effect variables to be considered here—achievement test scores and perception of liking by classmates. The reader is reminded that because the attitudinal variables primarily apply to children in grades 5-8, because of the low test-retest reliability for most of the Coleman attitude items, and also because of the differences on the items tapping attitudes between those posttested and those not posttested, it was decided to concentrate at this time on the two effect variables that apply to all the children in the two cohorts and to drop further analysis of the Coleman attitude scales, fate control and self-image.

In the previous chapter it was also revealed that there was further test attrition—not program attrition—in the 1967 cohort due to two factors not operative for the 1966 cohort: lack of parental consent to test and the discontinuance of several buses by the program staff in the spring of 1968. Thus, of the 69 children in the 1967 cohort who completed the year and had been pretested in September 1967 (O_2), 37 did not undergo posttesting in May 1968. As a result the investigator decided to ascertain if differences in O_2 responses (1967 cohort pretest in September 1967) existed between those posttested and those not posttested. Results of this analysis were presented in Chapter 5, and indicated that it was plausible to undertake the O_2-O_3 or longitudinal aspect of the study, at least with respect to achievement scores and perception of classmates' liking; the equivocal results for Coleman's fate control and self-image variables unfortunately militate against the employment of these two effect variables in the O_2-O_3 analysis. The foregoing considerations mean that there are 32 children available for the O_2-O_3 comparisons on two effect variables. The first of these two change analyses, on reading achievement test placement, is presented in Table 10.

ACHIEVEMENT CHANGE

The finding that the 1967 cohort improved its performance on the reading achievement test between pre- and posttest (Tables 10 and 11) provides corroboration for the difference found between O_1 and O_2 (see Table 6). Indeed, the mean difference found in the O_2-O_3 comparison is not only in the expected direction ($O_2 < O_3$) but is of a stronger magnitude than that found in the O_1-O_2 analysis, where, as expected, $O_2 < O_1$. It is emphasized that the mean score of 3.8 for the O_2 in Table 6 is precisely the same as the mean score for O_2 in Table 10. This is further evidence, it seems, that those who dropped out did not differ in reading ability from those who remained in the study and were posttested. The significance test for correlated means was employed and shows the O_2-O_3 difference (as presented in Table 11) to be statistically significant at the .05 level. The fact that the test-retest reliability (on two different forms) was good also buttresses the conclusion that the Exodus busing program resulted in substantial

TABLE 10

Distribution of Reading Stanine Positions on
O_2 and O_3, 1967 Cohort (N = 30)*

Stanine (Reading)	Time 1 (O₂)		Time 2 (O₃)	
	N	Percent	N	Percent
Two	6	20.0	2	6.7
Three	8	26.7	9	30.0
Four	5	16.6	7	23.3
Five	9	30.0	7	23.3
Six	2	6.7	3	10.0
Seven	—	—	2	6.7
Totals	30	100.0	30	100.0
	$\overline{X} = 3.8$		$\overline{X} = 4.2$	

*Two cases of incomplete test at Time 2 were not included in this analysis.

TABLE 11

Cross-Tabulation of Reading Stanines of
O_2 by O_3, 1967 Cohort (N = 30)

O_2 \ O_3 →	2	3	4	5	6	7	
2		3	3				6
3	2	3	1	2			8
4		2	1	2			5
5		1	2	3	1	2	9
6				2			2
	2	9	7	7	3	2	30

Time 1 (O_2) $\overline{X} = 3.8$; Time 2 (O_3) $\overline{X} = 4.2$
Using the test for correlated means,
t = 1.905 (d.f. = 29), P < .05, one tailed test.

improvement in reading achievement during one school year. I wish to explore this change in reading achievement further, but before doing so I would like to deal with another pressing issue.

While this finding of difference between O_2-O_3 confirms the O_1-O_2 comparison and thus rules out selection as a rival hypothesis, the reader will recall from Chapter 5 that differences found so far do not rule out maturation as a rival hypothesis. Since the study group is heterogeneous with respect to grade, however, it was thought that further analysis of the data by grade might help to clarify whether or not maturation was responsible for the differences found. Thus the investigator decided to assess mean stanine position by grade on both the pre- and posttest for the 1967 cohort and to control for maturation effects. The results of the first analysis are presented in Table 12(a). Since the number of cases in each grade is small, and in some instances there is only one child in a grade category, the reader is cautioned against reading too much into the findings.

Table 12(a) shows that there is a direct relationship between grade and mean improvement in reading: the higher the grade, the greater the improvement in mean scores between O_2 and O_3. It is noted that this finding is different from the usual finding of increasing deterioration in reading for inner-city children as they advance in grade.[7]

The second of the two analyses involving grade level represents an attempt to control for maturation effects. This analysis involves, for the 1967 cohort, pairing and comparing the mean pretest (O_2) reading achievement score for each grade level beginning with grade 4 with the mean posttest (O_3) reading achievement score for the children in the next lowest grade; thus the mean pretest reading score (stanine) for grade 4 is to be compared with the mean posttest reading score for grade 3, and so on.

Thus I will be comparing more mature children just entering the program with less mature children who have experienced the program for a year. Should the children who have been in the program for a year consistently show the greater mean score, then maturation can be ruled out as the explanation.

Table 12(b) presents this comparison and shows that the children in the posttest column (O_3) who are less mature consistently show higher mean reading scores than children in the pretest column (O_2). In only one of the five comparisons does the more mature group have a higher mean score. Thus it would seem that maturation can be ruled out as an explanation for the improvement found in reading ability.

I would now like the reader to return to Table 11 so that we may further observe the change within the 1967 cohort. The cross-tabulation in Table 11 shows that 14/30 or 47 percent of the children elevated their stanine position during the year, 9/30 or 30 percent

TABLE 12a

Reading Achievements and Assessment of
Maturation Effects, 1967 Cohort (N=30)

	Mean Stanine at O_2 (Pretest)	Mean Stanine at O_3 (Posttest)	N	
Grade 3	4.2	3.8	(5)	-.4
Grade 4	3.6	3.9	(8)	+.3
Grade 5	2.6	3.0	(3)	+.4
Grade 6	3.5	4.3	(12)	+.8
Grade 7	2.0	3.0	(1)	+1.0
Grade 8	3.0	5.0	(1)	+2.0

TABLE 12b

Reading Achievement and Maturation Controlled,
1967 Cohort (N=30)

	Mean Stanine at O_2 (Pretest)			Mean Stanine at O_3 (Posttest)	
Grade 4	3.6	(8)	Grade 3	3.8	(5)
Grade 5	2.6	(3)	Grade 4	3.9	(8)
Grade 6	3.5	(12)	Grade 5	3.0	(3)
Grade 7	2.0	(1)	Grade 6	4.3	(12)
Grade 8	3.0	(1)	Grade 7	3.0	(1)

remained stationary, and 7/30 or 23 percent lost ground. Presumably, since all of the children who were in stanine two in September 1967 moved up and out of that lowly position, they moved up at the expense of some children who were more highly placed in September than in May. A further look at Table 11 shows that seven of the children increased their stanine position by two places, while only one child among those who lost ground lost as many as two stanine places. Such cases make it imperative to try to shed light on the process of decline as well as the process of improvement. While I do not have interaction process data involving the child and other persons, such as teachers, peers, or parents, I do have questionnaire responses from the children and interview responses from some of the parents, which can be utilized in an attempt to cast more light on the child's experiences. Thus a few of the cases wherein children showed improvement or deterioration will be presented below, with data from parent interviews and child questionnaire responses.

The Case of M.T. and E.T.

This case involves a brother and sister, each of whom dropped back in stanine position over the course of the year: M., the boy, 9 years of age at time of pretest, who declined from the third to the second stanine; E., the girl, was 11 years old at time of pretest and declined from the fourth to the third stanine. Both children were in the fourth grade at the time of pretest.

From the interview with the mother it was learned that she was 39 years old and the father was 42 years of age. The parents lived with their 11 children in a five-room rented house. The father, born in Detroit, had completed eight years of schooling and was employed as a mechanic at the time of the interview in September 1967. Mrs. T., born in Boston, had completed high school, and later on had also taken a business course. She did not have a job outside of her duties as mother of 11 children and housewife. The family has been living at its present address for 10 years; however, the mother intensely dislikes the neighborhood in which they live and is anxious to move. Indeed, although Mrs. T. knew more than ten of her neighbors by name, she had not visited any of them during the month before the first interview. She appears to be a social isolate, since she was not a member of any club nor did she join any club during the interval between interviews.

On a five-item scale of authoritarianism she gave three "authoritarian" responses and gave "don't know" responses to the other two items. On the five-point scale of anomia she gave three "anomic" responses; her responses to these items suggest that a rather somber and restrictive atmosphere characterized the home.

Mrs. T. indicated at the end of the school year that she was "much more satisfied with the children's educational experience this year as compared to the last year," despite the fact that both M. and E. deteriorated in reading ability. In fact, the mother indicated that both children were "doing better work in school this year" during the second parent interview in May 1968. At this second interview she also indicated that the children's "teachers were more helpful" this year.

In the pretest questionnaire completed by M. he reports having made a few white friends at school. On the Colvin Silhouette Test he circled the fourth silhouette, an indication that he felt fairly well accepted by his classmates. Such an interpretation may not be justifiable, however, in view of responses to questions tapping his experiences in class. He indicated on these questions (1) that many classmates are unfair, (2) that it is hard to make white friends, and (3) that he doesn't feel that he belongs in this school. Indeed, he also responds that he wants to "go to a different school next year."

M.'s sister E., while two years older than M., also attends the fourth grade, repeating from last year. E. indicated on the September questionnaire that she did not have any white friends, and on neither the first nor the second questionnaire did she rate herself on the scale of classmates' liking (the Colvin Silhouette Test). She indicated, however, that she liked her teacher—who was black—very much.

It would seem that a number of factors may have interfered with these children's ability to do well at school. These would certainly include a very crowded home, with probably little opportunity to study in a quiet corner, although the mother's authoritarianism might well stem from a wish to produce better conditions for studying. It also seems that the mother's dislike of the neighborhood and her tendency to isolate herself could have resulted in the children's being cut off from certain experiences vital to their development. Such a withdrawn posture might also have contributed to E.'s failure to make any friends at school and to M.'s feelings that he didn't belong at the school to which he was bused by Exodus. Since both children and mother indicated satisfaction with teachers during the year, it is likely that the source of the children's academic problems lies elsewhere. If so, it seems unlikely that the children could profit from attendance at predominantly white schools.

The Case of J.R.

This was another child whose reading achievement score declined during the year, from stanine 5 to 3. Unfortunately Mrs. R. refused to allow herself to be interviewed, though, paradoxically perhaps, she permitted J. to participate in the study. Thus J.'s responses to questionnaire items allow the investigator to sketch some of the factors in his home and school experiences that may have affected his academic performance.

J. attended the third grade and was ten years old at the time of first questionnaire administration in September. He indicated that there was no father in the home and that ten other people besides himself lived in a rented seven-room house. J. felt that his classmates "didn't like him" after three weeks in the Exodus school and gave himself the worst possible rating—10—on the Colvin Silhouette Test. Although he thought highly of his teacher at the new school, who was white, he indicated in this September questionnaire that he "would like to go to a different school next year." By May, however, he indicated that "most of his classmates liked him" and his self-rating on the Colvin Test improved from least liked to a middle rating of 5. Another indication of this growing feeling of acceptance was highlighted in his May responses when he indicated that he was no longer sure that he wanted "to go to a different school next year." His end-of-the-year responses about his class indicated that the "teacher gives everyone a chance," that "the children are polite," and that he felt he "belonged in this class." Those responses include many departures in a positive direction from a once-gloomy outlook for this child.

While J. deteriorated in his first year in the program, a follow-up might show academic improvement, inasmuch as he learned to get along with his classmates and grew to feel accepted by them during his first year in a predominantly white school. His decline in reading ability may have come about because of his uncertainty and fears about being accepted by white classmates, fears that may have led him to concentrate his efforts on getting along with his peers, to the detriment of his classwork.

The Case of S.W.

This girl, 11 years of age and attending the sixth grade, advanced from the second to the fourth stanine during her first year in the program. She lives with her parents and two siblings in a rented house. The family has moved once in the past five years, and the mother states that she likes the neighborhood. Mrs. W. sees her neighbors frequently and is nonauthoritarian. Both parents are high school graduates and the father has had further training as a minister. Both parents were born in the Boston area and have lived here most of their lives. Mrs. W. was 41 years of age and the father was 43 at the time of pretest. During both interviews conducted with the mother, Mrs. W. indicated that her primary reason for busing was to obtain a quality education for her daughter. When asked to rank 11 items presumed to be indicators of a quality education, she incated that the "teacher-pupil ratio" was the single most important aspect of a quality education, followed by "individual attention from the teacher." At the end of the year the mother expressed great satisfaction with the child's school experience and made favorable comments about the teachers and about friends her daughter had acquired.

The girl, S., confirmed the mother's impressions and indicated at the beginning of the year that she got along well with teachers and peers. S. also indicated, in September, that she wanted to remain at this school next year. She indicated further that her parents push her to do well at school, and in the first questionnaire she agreed that she was "one of the best students in class." Interestingly, at the end of the year, having shown improvement in reading ability, S. felt that she was "an average student in her class." Also at the end of the year she was not so sure that her classmates liked her, and indicated that she "would like to go to a different school next year"—and this after agreeing that she has "learned more this year than any earlier year."

Thus while S. improved on the test of reading achievement, she is apparently disappointed in her relations with her peers. Perhaps this case suggests that some children can perform well academically in spite of—or because of—difficulties in peer relations. Readers should note the interesting and striking contrast with the case of J.R., where the reverse occurred: the child deteriorated on the reading test but showed progress in his peer relations.

The Case of N.C.

This 11-year-old sixth-grade boy was one of those who advanced two stanine positions during the year, moving from the fifth to the seventh stanine, and from a grade equivalence of 6.6 to a grade 10 equivalence. This is another instance where the mother could not be interviewed, so the case analysis depends on data obtained from the child. N. lived with both parents and had two siblings, neither of whom was involved with the Exodus program. Both parents worked, but N. said he did not know what kind of work his father did, nor did he know how much schooling the parents had had. Like most of the families involved, this one seemed to possess most of the standard conveniences: television, telephone, and hi-fi, but they did not own an automobile. On both the pre- and postquestionnaires this child showed strong feelings of fate control, giving the "control" answer for all three items on both occasions. Responses to the substitute self-image items also indicated a strong positive self-image at both times. Consistency of response further characterized N.'s feelings on the Colvin Silhouette Test, where he indicated that he felt he was fairly well liked by classmates, rating himself as a "4" on both occasions. He indicated that he had a few white friends but that not as many of his classmates liked him as he would wish. N. was very enthusiastic—again on both occasions—about his teachers at school and felt that they explained things clearly, were fair, and took a real interest in all the students. Like S.W., N. says he's "learned more this year than any earlier year." Also like S.W., N. says he's not sure that he would like to stay at his present school. Since he likes the teachers and did well academically, it seems wise to see if his peer relations account for his ambivalence about staying at his present school. N. indicated at both times some uncertainty about his classmates' attitudes; thus he was "not sure" if many of his classmates were fair. He deteriorated on a question that tapped trust: his response changed from "yes" to "not sure" on "You can trust almost everyone in this class." These responses, when paired with his admission that not as many of his white classmates liked him as he hoped he would like him, suggests that his peer relations may be bothering him a bit and may be responsible for some uncertainty about remaining at his present school.

N.C., like S.W., improved greatly in academic performance, but apparently is thinking seriously of going to another school due to a need for easier or better peer relations. While no conclusions about these few cases can be generalized, it is instructive to see the complexities and varieties of variable relationships that exist in them. It is especially noteworthy that this and the last case show the children getting along with teachers but despairing, apparently, about peer relationships.

The Case of J.B.

J. is a 12-year-old boy attending the sixth grade at the time of initial testing in September; he advanced from the second to the fourth stanine by the posttest in early June. J. also moved from reading at a grade equivalence of 3.8 in September to reading at a grade equivalence of 5.7 in June.

J. was the oldest of seven children, all living with their parents in a rented house. The mother stayed home with her children and the father worked as a maintenance man. J.'s mother was born in Tennessee and his father in South Carolina, and the family had been living in Boston since 1958. Mrs. B. said during the interview that they had been living at their present address for four years, that she liked the neighborhood in which they resided, and that they planned to remain in it. Thus, although Mrs. B. indicated that she did not get out to visit neighbors or relatives (perhaps because of her small children), the family appeared to be residentially stable. Both parents had a tenth-grade education.

Mrs. B. appeared to be a strict disciplinarian, agreeing with four of the five Srole questions tapping authoritarianism. She also appeared to be somewhat pessimistic (perhaps realistically) about life, agreeing with each of the five items tapping anomie. Mrs. B. indicated that she bused her child so that he might obtain a better education, inasmuch as she didn't think he had been progressing in his work at the previous school. During the first interview in October Mrs. B. said that she was quite satisfied with the progress that J. was making in the new school, but at the end-of-the-year interview she said she felt that her son's schoolwork hadn't greatly improved (although my tests indicated that J. had made substantial reading improvement).

For his part, J. felt at both the pre- and posttest that the teachers at the new school were really interested in him and that they were fairminded. At the time of pretest he thought that it was easy to make friends with classmates, although he also thought "many children in this class are not fair." Neither of these questions were answered by J. in June. While he did not complete the rating of his classmates' liking for him in September, by June he felt that he was well liked by his classmates. At both times J. agreed with the statement "I work hard in school but don't seem to get anywhere"; thus he seems to share his mother's pessimistic outlook on life. (Unfortunately J. did not respond to any of the Coleman items at either time.)

J.B. is a boy who apparently has made tremendous strides in his academic work but can't admit yet that life will offer him any chance for success. (This may be a pretty realistic appraisal from the viewpoint of a black child.) J.'s mother doesn't feel that he has improved much but somehow she feels that the new school is better. J. is working hard but doesn't feel he is getting anywhere. Yet, although J. indicates that he doesn't like school in general, he also thought at the end of the school year that he had "learned more this year than any earlier year." Moreover, J. started off the year indicating that he wanted to leave school at the end of high school, but at the posttest he agreed with the statement "I want to go to college." It seems to me that J. and his mother both are tentatively hopeful that J. will improve in his school work and in his chances for success, but that they are also guarded in their verbally expressed expectations. Although I do not have any direct evidence that J.'s grades have improved (and his mother was interested in grades), I would hazard the guess that his own estimate that he had "learned more this year than any earlier year" will certainly increase his motivation to work hard at school and may well result in improved grades at the new school in subsequent years. His mother's apparent authoritarian personality will undoubtedly help J. in his persistence at school.

CHANGES IN CHILD'S PERCEPTION OF CLASSMATES' LIKING FOR HIM

The change analysis for the second effect variable—child's perception of extent to which his classmates like him—is presented in Tables 13 and 14.

Tables 13 and 14 show that the O_2-O_3 difference is not in the expected direction; it had been expected that the children would have felt better liked by their classmates after an academic year's experience in the integrated setting, but such is not the case. The children actually deteriorated; at the end of the year proportionately fewer of them felt well liked (positions 1 to 5), and more of them did not know how their classmates felt about them. The exception to this trend is that fewer of the Time 2 children felt poorly liked (positions 6 to 10).

95

TABLE 13

Distribution of Child's Responses to Colvin
Silhouette Test, O_2 and O_3, 1967 Cohort (N = 29)*

Rating Perception of Classmates' Liking	Time 1 (O_2)		Time 2 (O_3)	
	N	Percent	N	Percent
One (best liked)	6	20.8	2	6.9
Two	—	—	—	—
Three	—	—	1	3.4
Four	3	10.3	3	10.3
Five	4	13.8	4	13.8
Six	3	10.3	2	6.9
Seven	1	3.4	—	—
Eight	1	3.4	—	—
Nine	2	6.9	—	—
Ten (least liked)	4	13.8	1	3.4
Don't know	5	17.3	16	55.3
Total	29	100.0	29	100.0

*Three tests left blank.

This last observation, however, is accounted for in part by a shift
from feeling poorly liked at Time 1 to not knowing how classmates felt
at Time 2 (see Table 13). On balance, these data not only do not support findings from the O_1-O_2 comparison, where a year in the program
resulted in more children feeling well liked (see Table 7), but actually,
go against results of the O_1-O_2 comparison. While it had been assumed
that such an unexpected result might reflect on the selection process,
the expected O_2-O_3 difference on achievement as well as the lack of
evidence that background factors differed between the two cohorts
(Table 5) seem to argue against attribution of the present finding to
selection. One of the reasons for the reversal, it seems, might lie
with the problem of test attrition, since slightly more of the best-liked
children and also more of the "don't knows" in the 1967 cohort were
not posttested and thus were not available for the present O_2-O_3
analysis. It may also be that the continuing turmoil in Boston over
school racial integration, growing concern in the black community
over the politics of education as it affected black children, and coolness
towards school integration among whites had an effect on the children;
perhaps the children were not left alone by the adults—black and

white—and perhaps the process, so typical of children, of getting acquainted either did not take place or, if it did occur, did not result in feelings of being well-liked by very many classmates.

Again, it is unfortunate that this matter cannot be resolved. It is hazardous to speculate about a process of alienation going on among the children when the finding could be explained by attrition, by unreliability, by selection, or by some other source of invalidity. Perhaps it is enough to let the matter rest here, and to add the suggestion that further research on the role of changes in perception of self by others as well as on other attitudinal components in programs of this kind needs to be undertaken.

In sum, the main finding we are left with from the O_1-O_2 and O_2-O_3 analysis presented here on the children in Exodus is that there was a significant improvement in reading achievement and that this improvement is due to the Exodus program. I was unable to find any

TABLE 14

Cross-Tabulation of Responses to Colvin Silhouette
Test, O_2 by O_3, 1967 Cohort (N = 29)

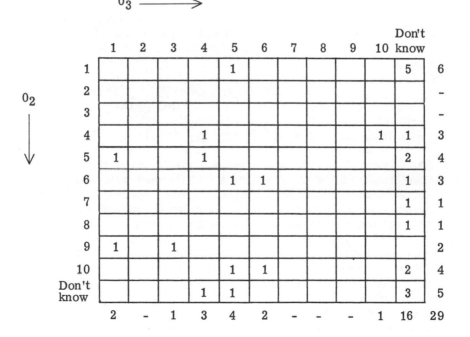

$O_3 \longrightarrow$

	1	2	3	4	5	6	7	8	9	10	Don't know	
1					1						5	6
2												-
3												-
4				1						1	1	3
5	1			1							2	4
6					1	1					1	3
7											1	1
8											1	1
9	1		1									2
10					1	1					2	4
Don't know				1	1						3	5
	2	-	1	3	4	2	-	-	-	1	16	29

O_2 (down)

strong relationships in an attempt to explicate this finding; perhaps the improvement in reading achievement was the result of multiple factors, some of which were measured in the study and others not. Certainly it was unfortunate that data on parent and teacher attitudes and behavior either could not be collected or, if collected, could not be fully employed in the analysis of data.

The investigator has already indicated why parent and home factors could not be utilized in connection with the data from children, and this was most unfortunate. Neither was the educational or political atmosphere such that it led the investigator to attempt early in the design of research to collect data from the children's teachers. Indeed, in 1966 the school superintendent refused to provide the investigator with the grades of Exodus children. When the air cleared somewhat and the school board agreed to cooperate in such an enterprise, it was too late to obtain funding support for proposed research on the children's teachers. So the research reported on here was admittedly not as comprehensive as the investigator had hoped it would be.

Because of the paucity of research data from projects such as Exodus, however, the researcher will present limited aggregate findings from the parent data collected during interviews at the end of the 1967-68 school year. While the parent data lost one of its most valuable functions when the investigator was unable to utilize it as a source of independent variables in connection with the data on the children, it seems useful to present at least a few findings and impressions gained from contacts with the parents. This report on the parents is intended to extend the scope of knowledge about program effects.

PARENTS' VIEW OF THE BUSING PROGRAM

At the end of the 1967-68 school year all available parents were reinterviewed in what were referred to as "repeat" interviews The largest block of questions focused on the parents' own "evaluation" (impressions) of the usefulness of the operation as a whole and the particular effects on their own children. These questions were designed to facilitate comparisons between the parents of the 1966 and 1967 cohorts.[8] Thus the parents' data presented here are intended for use in a suggestive way only in the amplification of comparative effects of the busing program on the children in the 1966 and 1967 cohorts. Moreover, because the data are used only in a suggestive way, data are presented on all those parents who cooperated in the repeat interview, even if, as in some cases, posttest data on their children had not been obtained.

During January 1967 78 new Exodus parents (of the 1966 cohort) were interviewed. Of these, 56 had children in grades 3-8. At the time of the repeat interview in May 1968, some 16 months later, dropouts, interview refusals, and not-locatables resulted in the re-interview of only 34 of these 56 parents. Also, during the 1967-68 academic year 63 new Exodus parents (of the 1967 cohort) were interviewed, and all of these parents had at least one child in one of the grades between 3 and 8. At the time "repeat" interviews were held (May 1968) eight months had elapsed, and because of dropouts, refusals, and a few who could not be reached, only 43 of the 63 could be reinterviewed. Thus, due to the interview attrition problem, it is emphasized that the parent data must be viewed cautiously.

The first evaluative question asked of the parents during the repeat interview was "In general, compared with last year, how satisfied are you with your child's experience this year?" Respondents were asked to answer in terms of a five-point scale: (1) much more satisfied this year, (2) somewhat more satisfied this year, (3) about the same degree of satisfaction, (4) somewhat less satisfied this year, and (5) much less satisfied this year. The distribution of these responses, some of which are collapsed, are presented in Table 15.

The distribution of responses shows a modest tendency for the parents of the 1967 cohorts, who spent "last year" in a predominantly black school, to be more satisfied with the school experience "this year" than parents of the 1966 cohort. This finding seems plausible since the question is a comparative one (this year versus last year), and the 1967 cohort parents were new to the program "this year" and perhaps inclined to justify their decision. Of course, it would be equally plausible if the 1966 parents had been more satisfied "this year,"

TABLE 15

Distribution of Parent Responses to the Question "How
satisfied are you with your child's (children's)
educational experience this year?"

	1966 Parents (N=34)		1967 Parents (N=43)	
	N	Percent	N	Percent
Somewhat or much more satisfied this year	18	52.9	27	62.8
About the same	11	32.4	12	27.9
Somewhat or much less satisfied this year	5	14.7	4	9.3
Total	34	100.0	43	100.0

since one could have attributed that result to a shaking down or adjustment process during the first year in the program. Since the difference
is rather small anyway, it is likely that both the "real" process of
adjusting and the "mental" process of justification were going on.

Parents were asked several other questions about the child's
school experience this year compared to last year. One of these questions asked whether the child "got along better with teachers this year."
A second asked if the child was "doing better schoolwork." On neither
of these questions was there any difference in response between cohort
years: 47 percent of 1966 parents and 44 percent of 1967 parents responded affirmatively to the first question and 50 percent and 56 percent
responded affirmatively to the second.

Taking a slightly different tack, we then inquired about the number
of white friends the children had at school. This question is of interest
since earlier in this chapter (see Table 13) data was presented that
showed some deterioration over the year in the extent to which children
in the 1967 cohort felt they were liked by (white) classmates. The
distribution of parent responses to this question is presented in Table 16.

The data shown in Table 16 seem consistent with those presented
in Table 13. Thus, in Table 13 about 34 percent of the children (at
O_3) rated themselves from 1 to 5 (or in the somewhat-to-best-liked
range), while in Table 16 about 32 percent of the parents of the 1967
cohort indicate that their children have one or more white friends.
Again, in Table 13 55 percent of the children state that they don't know
how well liked they are; a strikingly similar proportion of parents (60
percent) state that they don't know how many white friends their child
has. Responses of the parents of the 1966 cohort are most consistent
with the distribution of children on the Colvin Silhouette Test at O_2.
At a minimum, these response similarities of the parent and child
cohorts suggest that the children were saying the same things to
their parents that they were indicating to the testers. If they are
taken at face value, it is quite apparent that for the children in the
1967 cohort the 1967-68 academic year was not a good one for getting
along easily with white classmates (Tables 13 and 16). In contrast,
the responses of parents of the 1966 cohort indicate that their children
are much more likely to have made friends among their white classmates. It must be kept in mind, however, that the 1966 cohort children
have had twice as long to develop friendships as the children in the
1967 cohort. Thus it would seem, as far as the parent responses
indicate, that the making of acquaintances takes time and that by the
end of another year the children in the 1967 cohort will have acquired
more white friends.

Another question put to the parents was "Over-all, do you think
that school integration is helpful or harmful to black children?" The
parents overwhelmingly felt that school integration was helpful:

TABLE 16

Distribution of parent responses to the question "How
many white friends does your child have at school?"*

	1966 Parents	(N=34)	1967 Parents	(N=43)
	N	Percent	N	Percent
None	—	—	3	7.0
One or several	21	61.8	8	18.6
A lot	5	14.7	6	13.9
Don't know	8	23.5	26	60.5
Total	34	100.0	43	100.0

*Responses given for the oldest child where there was more than
one child from the family in the program.

94 percent and 97 percent respectively of parents in the 1966 and 1967
cohort years gave the "helpful" response. Since these parents had
all volunteered for the program, it is perhaps not surprising that
their evaluation of school integration was positive. Still, it is always
possible that even volunteers for a program will decide after one or
two years that the program is doing more harm than good. Indeed,
some of the parents who felt that the program had harmful effects had
already removed their children by the time of the repeat interview
(see Chapter 5). Still, a large majority of the parents and children
remained in the program, and nearly all of the parents who participated
in the interview indicated that it was helpful. Some of the specific
reasons parents gave in response to a request to elaborate on what it
was about the program that was helpful are contained in the following
quoted statements:

> "I feel that if she were not with this program, some of
> the subjects she is taking she would not have had." (Moth-
> er of a sixth-grader.)

> "They meet more children of different variety, like a
> melting pot, and understand other people's customs."
> (Mother of a fourth-grader and a sixth-grader.)

> "The program is helpful because [he is] able to see other
> things and to want something more and better than they
> see in our neighborhood." (Mother of a fifth-grader.)

"There is more concern from the teachers." (Mother of a fifth-grader.)

"[She is] preparing herself to compete in the outside world." (Mother of a third-grader.)

"She enjoys more things. She talks about things which she never talked about before." (Mother of a seventh-grader.)

"[The program is helpful] because the teachers are going to teach the white students in the classroom so I know my kid will receive the same quality education." (Mother of a fourth-grader.)

In spite of the mothers' laudatory statements about the good effects of the program, it certainly should not be assumed that the Exodus children had only pleasant experiences in the predominantly white schools in which they were recently enrolled. Thus, when the parents were asked to report on and describe the extent and nature of any "prejudice which your child has experienced at school," approximately 20 percent and 15 percent respectively of the 1966 and 1967 parents reported that their child had encountered prejudice at school during the 1967-68 school year. Some of the mothers' remarks about this matter were as follows:

"Sometimes even with the teacher there is a little prejudice. The Negro child messed up her paper and the teacher would not give her another. The white child messed up her paper and the teacher gave her another sheet. Sometimes she raises her hand and is not given a chance to answer. She says she will continue to raise her hand until she is answered." (Mother of a sixth-grader, 1966 cohort.)

"He was standing at the water fountain when a white kid came by and knocked his books down and then smiled. So they had a fight. The principal told him that the next time he gets into a fight he would be thrown out of school." (Mother of an eighth-grader, 1967 cohort.)

"There was some name-calling by classmates. He is the only Negro in his room." (Mother of a third-grader, 1967 cohort.)

"There has been only one incident: She found a note in her desk saying 'Nigger you stink." (Mother of a seventh-grader, 1966 cohort.)

"A [white] mother came up to school and put my child up against a wall and threatened her because of a disturbance between two children, hers and mine. The teacher saw it and interceded on behalf of my child." (Mother of a fifth-grader, 1966 cohort.)

These statements suggest that there were enough unpleasant experiences to keep Exodus parents from relaxing very much and, indeed, to cause some of the Exodus parents considerable concern. Moreover, as indicated in Chapter 5, some of the parents in each cohort year withdrew their children from the busing program. It is also true, however, that there were other reasons besides the encountering of racial prejudice or discrimination that led some of the parents to withdraw their children, such as fighting between black children on the Exodus buses and problems with younger children. Still, in spite of the variety of problems that parents and their children encountered, nearly all of the parents, including most of those whose children encountered racial prejudice, indicated that they found the program valuable for their children.

The data from the parent interviews, even though it could not be directly utilized with the data obtained from the children, has been presented because it was felt that parent data findings would be useful in the corroboration and elucidation of findings on the children. The results of analysis of parent data do seem to be consistent with those proceeding from analysis of data from children. Thus, the fact that the parents seem pleased with the program may stem to some degree from the gains made on achievement test scores by the Exodus children; similarly, parents in the 1967 cohort seem to be in the dark— and skeptical—about the extent to which their children have acquired white friends, a finding consistent with the considerable profession of ignorance by 1967 cohort children about how well liked they are. On balance, it seems reasonable to conclude that, as far as academic performance is concerned, the parents' responses as well as the results of achievement testing suggest that significant gains were made by the children during their first year in the program. Many parents also seemed to indicate that the educational opportunities were greater in the predominantly white schools. However, when we considered the affective component, mixed results were found. The cross-sectional analysis (Table 7) produced results indicating that children in Exodus developed "feelings of acceptance by classmates" during their first year in the program, but this was not supported by results of the longitudinal analysis. It was suggested that this reversal in the long-itudinal data could be due to any one or more of several possibilities, including selection, test attrition, and school atmosphere. Certainly, more evaluative research on programs intended to further school racial integration seems called for. Moreover, other criteria of program success besides cognitive gains should be considered. In the present study I have attempted to do this by focusing on several affective components of success in addition to achievement scores. There is one other indicator of program success that will be discussed in this report. This had to do with the activities and changes that took place among Exodus activists—parents who played a leading part in the organization. These changes and activities, of both a group and an individual nature, will be discussed briefly in the following chapter.

NOTES

1. For a fuller exposition see Campbell and Stanley, Experimental and Quasi-Experimental Designs for Research (Chicago: Rand McNally, 1966). For detailed description of the problems in the present study see Chapters 4 and 5.

2. James Coleman, et.al., Equality of Educational Opportunity (Washington, D.C.: U.S. Government Printing Office, 1966).

3. See Irwin Katz, "A Critique of Personality Approaches to Negro Performance, With Research Suggestions," Journal of Social Issues, XXV, (Summer 1969), pp. 13-27.

4. Ibid., pp. 13-27.

5. Ibid., p. 25.

6. Coleman, et al, op. cit., pp. 319-23.

7. For example, see Kenneth Clark, "Alternative Public School Systems," Harvard Educational Review, XXXVIII (Winter, 1968), pp. 100-113.

8. For comparison between the 1965 and 1966 parents see James E. Teele and Clara Mayo, "School Racial Integration: Tumult and Shame," Journal of Social Issues, XXV (January 1969), pp. 137-156, also in Howard Gadlin and Bertram Garskof, The Uptight Society: A Book of Readings (Belmont, Calif.: Brooks/Cole, 1970).

7

THE GROWTH
AND DEVELOPMENT
OF EXODUS PARENTS

I do not know how many black long-time residents of Boston would agree, but one black leader recently commented that "the most exciting development in the black community [Roxbury] in the last twenty years was the development of Operation Exodus." Perhaps many of Boston's black population undoubtedly would agree with this sentiment. The list of both organizational and individual accomplishments by the parents who formed Operation Exodus is massive. In this chapter I shall present a few of these achievements, beginning with what was undoubtedly the most signal accomplishment of the parents: their coming together and organizing themselves into an effective group or association in the face of many difficulties. A part of this history was presented in Chapter 1, which chronicled the immediate background of events leading up to Exodus. Now I shall extend that dimension and also attempt to place the organization and development of Exodus in sociological perspective.

ORGANIZATIONAL ACHIEVEMENT: BLACK FAMILIES AND THE EDUCATIONAL BUREAUCRACY[1]

In a novel statement, utilizing an admittedly exaggerated characterization, Litwak and Meyer[2] have pointed out a striking paradox of the relationship between bureaucracies and primary groups: while the instrumental styles and patterns of bureaucratic organizations are antithetical to the affective mode that underlies the primary group (e.g., the family), the two forms (bureaucracy and primary group) remain in contact with each other. Given the difference between the two, students of organizations have implied that they will do best not to overlap and in fact to avoid each other (Parsons, 1959). Litwak and Meyer, however, show that they do not usually remain isolated from each other in modern industrial society and that there is substantial contact between them. Litwak and Meyer address themselves to the "motivation" for this contact (attainment of common goals via unique features of each); in addition, they describe mechanisms that are employed by both bureaucracies and primary groups in initiating and sustaining communication with each other. The authors indicate that, because of their essential differences in style and purpose, optimum contact between the two is attained when they are neither too distant nor too close to each other. Thus Litwak and Meyer employ a balance model.*

In describing some of the coordinating mechanisms distinguishable within the literature on social organization but which have not previously been explicitly acknowledged to be involved in the coordination between bureaucracies and external primary groups, Litwak and Meyer approach the mechanisms from the perspective of the bureaucracy but indicate that the same or similar mechanisms are available to primary groups. The coordinating mechanisms are (1) detached expert, (2) opinion leader, (3) settlement house, (4) voluntary association, (5) common messenger, (6) mass media, (7) formal authority, and (8) delegated function. Principles of communication governing the operation of these mechanisms are then described. These principles are focused on narrowing or increasing the social distance between bureaucracies and primary groups, and govern the extent of initiative, the intensity of relations, the complexity of communication, ant the extensiveness of communication. Finally, Litwak and Meyer also describe and discuss the various types and complexities of bureaucratic organizations and how the type of organization enters into the selection of coordinating mechanisms. They then generate hypotheses about balance and goal achievement by interrelating type of bureaucracy, type of primary group, and mechanisms of coordination.

Litwak and Meyer acknowledge that their presentation is not meant to be exhaustive and that they have presented only a first attempt to study a neglected but important problem in the understanding of contemporary society. In their closing statement they point out several research and theoretical areas that need to be taken up. One

-----

* Later on they describe ways in which their balance model differs from that of Heider and others. Obviously, Litwak and Meyer's approach differs from that of the psychologists in dealing with interorganizational behavior rather than intra- and interpersonal perception and behavior. In addition, while Heider and others dealt with how consistency leads to contact, Litwak and Meyer deal with how contact is initiated or maintained despite inconsistencies in major aspects of the situation.

of these areas, which constitutes the focus of the present discussion, is the initiation of community contact by the primary group. The authors suggest that initiation by primary groups might be different from those by bureaucracies: the bureaucracy, since it has great resources, can initiate community contact with almost any mechanism of coordination; by contrast, the primary group can start only with those mechanisms that require minimum resources. From the experiences of the present author Litwak and Meyer seem correct in hypothesizing that the primary group is more likely to resort to the formation of a voluntary association.

It would seem that the number of resources available affects the likelihood of whether or not a given coordinating mechanism will work and that these resources may differ only in degree for the educational bureaucracy and the primary group. The resources will include power, knowledge, and invulnerability to pressure. They are discussed here from the perspective of the primary group vis-à-vis the educational bureaucracy.

Power: If the primary group has considerable influence—i.e., the ability to win allies—it has power, and the question then is whether or not it can use its power appropriately via a coordinating mechanism to attain sufficient communication and balance with the educational bureaucracy and a subsequent movement toward the desired educational goal.

Knowledge: If the primary group has adequate information on the way the bureaucracy works and of the formal and informal regulations governing the bureaucratic operations, presumably this knowledge will assist it in attempting to communicate with officials in the bureaucracy.

Invulnerability: The primary group may have power and knowledge and still fail to attain a balanced relationship with the bureaucracy if it is vulnerable to pressures arising from the efforts of a competing primary group that is also attempting to effect communication with the bureaucracy. In a sense, it is the vulnerability of the bureaucracy to the latter group's desire for linkage that may inhibit linkage by the first primary group.

One does indeed wonder what happens when the coordinating mechanism employed by a primary group fails to achieve the desired communication with the bureaucracy. The parents who later formed Operation Exodus were pushed into action by the failure of the educational officials to respond to their requests to improve educational opportunities for their children.

These early "requests" included a good number of school stay-outs, parent marches, picketing of the School Committee building, and other short-term demonstrations.* All of the demonstrations, as stated before, were organized in protest of double sessions, crowded classrooms, teacher turnover in inner city schools, shortages of books, and school curricula.

It is likely that from the point of view of the educational authorities the parents who were demanding improvements lacked the requisite power to force officials to take them seriously. The School Department was under the control of the School Committee, a body of elected officials; repeatedly, black parents found that a majority of the school committeemen were inclined to make decisions that were politically expedient and counter to the parents' demands for better teachers, less overcrowding, and so on. Consistent with the view that the parents lacked power was the fact that those candidates for office who were in favor of school improvements and school integration usually were not elected to the School Committee between 1962 and 1968.

The parents demonstrated that they had substantial knowledge of the working of the bureaucracy, but this knowledge did them little good against the power of the School Committee. Finally, the parents were vulnerable to the competing demands of those who were opposed to any movement toward school integration. Indeed, it was awareness of their vulnerability and relative lack of power to influence the School Committee that led the parents to form a voluntary association, known first as the Roxbury-North Dorchester Parent Association and later as Operation Exodus.

Litwak and Meyer's formulation suggests that vulnerability and lack of power may result in the failure of the primary group to attain optimum communication with the bureaucracy. This formulation suggests several consequences that might have flowed from the failure of the unorganized parents to enter into meaningful communication with school officials. First, the parents might have altered their goals. (In some communities, where balanced communication was often not possible between black primary groups and the educational bureaucracies, many black families learned not to pursue the educational goals they wanted for their children and instead scaled down their goals to the levels set for them by the powerful educational bureaucracies.) Second, the parents could have entered into prolonged or periodic conflict with the educational bureaucracy. Third, the

---

*A chronology of these short-term demonstrations was presented in Chapter 1. It is notable that the events in Boston in the 1960s, just as those in the 1840s, led to state legislation that focused on school integration.

parents might have withdrawn from their effort to establish meaningful communication with the school officials.

Instead of any of these, the parents under discussion decided to organize themselves into an association in order to pursue the educational goals they had set for their children. While the parents did not withdraw altogether from communication with school officials, neither did they continue to make frontal assaults on members of the School Committee. Instead the group proceeded to make use of Boston's open enrollment policy in transporting their children at their own expense to schools they assumed would provide better educational opportunities for their children. While they did not alter their goals, neither did they enter into further prolonged controversy with school officials over the problem of educating their children, a conflict that would have delighted the political demagogues. Instead the parents decided to slow down efforts to communicate with an intransigent bureaucracy, organized themselves, and orchestrated a privately funded busing operation that won many supporters, both black and white.

Once the parents had decided that formal organization was necessary, the process of organizing proceeded quickly and smoothly. It included the election of a slate of officers, election of a board of directors, renting and renovation (by the fathers in Exodus) of an office, obtaining of a staff (of volunteers, initially) to man the Exodus office, and incorporation as a nonprofit organization. Program activities, of course, started with the busing operation.

During this period the parents greatly developed their knowledge and expertise about various phases of the educational enterprise. Throughout, the parents were led by nonprofessionals, although they were not opposed to seeking advice from professionals—black or white—when they needed it. The staff of Operation Exodus, under the leadership of Mrs. Ellen Jackson, acquired much knowhow in educational matters. This knowhow was based on a growing awareness of the way educational bureaucrats make administrative decisions at the level of individual schools as well as of decision-making procedures in the School Department. Exodus became the premier educational organization in the black community if not in the whole city. Many parents whose children weren't even in the busing program and who attended neighborhood schools brought their school problems to the staff of Operation Exodus.

Once it became clear that Operation Exodus had expertise and community support, both academic and nonacademic, and that it was here to stay, the Boston School Department and, to a lesser degree, the Boston School Committee began to respond in a way predictable by the Litwak-Meyer formulation. The school officials began to deal with Operation Exodus, although in slow and limited ways. Slow in the sense that it took more than a year for positive communication to develop between the superintendent's office and Exodus; limited in the sense that this communication did not have to do with financial assistance for the busing program but with ways of enabling the black community to have a direct voice in the operation of schools in the black community. (It was not until 1969—four years after the initiation of Exodus—that any public funds were granted for the busing operation.) This rapprochement developed, it would seem, as a direct outgrowth of the growing prestige and influence (power) of the Exodus organization. The organization's records show informal contacts originating in late 1966 and involving representatives of Exodus, the Boston school superintendent's office, and interested local area academicians, who met frequently to explore ways of improving predominantly black schools and facilitating parent participation in these schools. Requests for such meetings were frequently made by the parents and ignored by the school officials between 1962 and 1966. The organization's success in engendering this contact was itself a major achievement. Moreover, by late 1966 communication between the writer and the superintendent's office concerning the cooperation of the school department in an evaluation of program effects had been renewed, and this time the superintendent had indicated a willingness to cooperate in the research endeavor.

If the parents in Operation Exodus had done nothing beyond the busing and related administrative activities, they would have accomplished much; in fact they did much more. Their record is a record of rational, goal-directed behavior; the parents consistently and over a protracted period directed their efforts to the facilitation of a quality education for their children. Over the years succeeding the initiation of the busing operation they were engaged in many educational enterprises. This involvement was consistent with one of the themes of the organization: the provision of alternatives for black parents striving to educate their children. Thus, for example, they were a leading force in the development of a network of privately operated community schools. They also gave direction and energy to the growing movement by blacks to gain some influence and control over the public schools in Roxbury. The extent to which the parents in Operation Exodus became involved in the attempt to provide educational alternatives for Roxbury was of such magnitude that it cannot be fully presented here;* however, their leadership in the development

----

*Other Exodus activities, some of which are only tangentially related to educational matters, were (1) a major role in efforts to curtail the Boston urban disorders during June 1968 and to harness

of a Community School Board may be observed in the following excerpt
from a report to the Exodus Board of Directors, dated April 23, 1968:

> As stated in the original proposal, Operation Exodus had
> begun the formation of a Community School Board in
> September of 1966 following a re-evaluation of program
> emphasis and orientation. The original objective was to
> organize parents in 14 districts in which there exist
> predominantly black schools. Parents in these 14 dis-
> tricts would organize local parent groups, each of which
> would elect representatives to the community-wide
> school board. The community-wide board would then con-
> sist of these representatives, plus some 10 unaffiliated or
> at large members elected by the original 24 local rep-
> resentatives. . . . [An initial] meeting was the beginning
> of a series of community meetings which represented
> extensive collaboration between organized sectors of the
> black community which, to that point, had not had the
> opportunity to communicate directly and to plan together
> for radical change, and unaffiliated parents interested or
> concerned about the education of their children.

It is apparent from the above that Exodus did not consider busing
to be a panacea but only one of several options that parents might
have in trying to broaden educational opportunities for their children.
It is also apparent that members of Operation Exodus were engaged
in teaching and organizing others for the purpose of improving the
quality of education. They were, indeed, educational stalwarts.

Many of these parents—nonprofessionals so to speak—proved
to be so talented that a great demand for their individual services
developed, and naturally this demand was most visible with regard to
the leaders of Exodus. Nearly always, when one views the staffs of
private schools and other educational organizations in Boston today,
one will find persons who got their start with Operation Exodus. In
the next few paragraphs I shall describe the development and some
of the accomplishments of a few of these Exodus leaders.

––––––––––––––––––

and redirect the energies of those involved; (2) the development by
the fathers in Exodus of a recreation program; (3) the creation of a
psychological counseling service staffed by psychologists from Boston
College and Boston University; (4) leadership in the development of
community interest in a school lunch program; and (5) organizing
community interest in physical and mental health facilities.

INDIVIDUAL ACHIEVEMENT

Mrs. Ellen Jackson, a Roxbury housewife with a daughter in the program, was and continues to be the president of Operation Exodus. A high school graduate, she has become one of the most dynamic leaders of any city and has a long list of accomplishments that verifies this assessment. While president of Exodus she also held an executive office with the National Association of Black Women. In 1969 she was appointed a Fellow in the Institute of Politics of Harvard University's John F. Kennedy School of Government and in 1970 became a degree candidate at the Harvard Graduate School of Education. In 1971 Mrs Jackson was named one of Boston's ten outstanding leaders by the Chamber of Commerce. Needless to say, she was and is the unquestioned leader of Exodus and the single most indispensable member of the organization.

Mrs. Betty Johnson was also a Roxbury housewife, with two years of high school, who became the cofounder and first vice president of the Roxbury-North Dorchester Parents Association (Exodus). She was the first of the administrative staff to leave Exodus for another community leadership position. Her move was occasioned by the development of The Metropolitan Educational Transportation Conference (METCO). Mrs. Johnson joined the METCO staff as a paid administrator at the end of the first year of Operation Exodus.

Mr. Frank Silva, a high school graduate, was the treasurer of Operation Exodus. He also one of the founders of the organization and had a son in Exodus. During the first three months of the program, in concert with other male parents, he helped in the major renovation of an old Blue Hill Avenue building, which became the headquarters of Exodus. While treasurer of Operation Exodus he enrolled in a work-study degree program at Northeastern University. He has to this day remained one of the mainstays of Exodus. As treasurer, and in close cooperation with other staff and board members, he was a major figure in the Exodus fundraising program.

Mr. Marvin Butler, a high school dropout with a daughter in Exodus, was the organizer and director of a communitywide recreational program for teenage boys in the black community, initiated in the early months of 1966. This program, under the egis of Operation Exodus and staffed by a number of adult males affiliated with Exodus, became most popular with the boys of Roxbury and North Dorchester. Mr. Butler subsequently resigned from his factory job to become recreation director at the Roxbury YMCA, continuing to work closely with the recreational and other programs at Exodus.

Mrs. Marlene McIlvaine, also a founder of Exodus, with two sons in the busing program, was a high school graduate. She was in charge of investigation of problems Exodus children had at school, ranging from academic difficulties to problems in relationships with teachers, principals, or peers. Because of her knowledge of the Exodus children and her interest in effects of the program, the investigator asked Mrs. McIlvaine if she would like to receive training in the coordination and administrative aspects of field research. She readily agreed, and later on the Exodus staff and board agreed to her appointment as field coordinator of research, where she worked closely with the investigator.

Mrs. Audrey Butler, wife of Marvin Butler, mother of four and a high school graduate, was one of the founders of Operation Exodus. With the inception of Exodus she became and has remained the office manager. She was in charge of all records maintained by Exodus and of office personnel. Like all the staff, she was paid only when money was available for salaries; when money was tight, staff members volunteered their services. Also like several of the other staff workers, Mrs. Butler had never held a job outside of the home previous to her work with Exodus.

Mrs. Gwenna Cummings was, to my knowledge, the only staff person at Exodus who had attended college, having completed one year. Joining the staff a few months after the program began, she became the director of the Exodus Tutorial Program, a year-round program open to any school-age child who requested help. She oriented and made assignments each year for several hundred children from the black community and for between 40 and 60 tutors, primarily undergraduates from the local colleges. Mrs. Cummings also initiated a cultural enrichment program under the egis of Operation Exodus. As with most of the programs run by Exodus, funds were not available for the cultural enrichment program and it was operated by volunteer workers. In 1968, three years after she began working for Exodus, Mrs. Cummings agreed to teach tutorial techniques and other subjects at the Boston State College for Teachers. At this time she began to divide her time between her teaching activities at Boston State and her activities at Exodus.

Mr. Richard Dennis, a high school graduate, had a son in the Exodus program. A founder of Exodus, Mr. Dennis was in the Navy and stationed in the Boston area during the first two years of the program. He was one of the parents trained by the investigator in interviewing techniques during the first phase of the research. Mr. Dennis became so skilled an interviewer that he was often used as a model in role-playing skits during interviewer training sessions.

Mrs. Jacqueline LeBeau, a high school dropout, joined Exodus during the first year's operation. During the 1966-67 academic year she was the Exodus representative to the Roxbury Community School Board, where she became a participant in all activities designed to give the black community some voice and influence in both the improvement and the operation of public and private schools in the black community. As time passed such activities took on more and more importance for the Exodus staff, which after all was primarily interested in maximizing educational opportunities for the community's children.

The list of Exodus personnel is quite long, and much more could be said of the activities and development of individual staff members. Only a few of them have been named, and only a small portion of the activities of those named has been catalogued. The full story of the growth and development of the individual board and staff members of Exodus remains to be told. My purpose in touching on this subject at all was to give the reader some flavor of the excitement of those years and of the deep motivation, dedication, and talent of the men and women who constituted Operation Exodus.

I also wished to call attention to the need for social scientists to diversify the indexes of achievement that we traditionally and typically employ in evaluative research. Nowhere is this need more visible than in our reliance on indexes of "achievement" and cognitive development in the evaluation of educational programs. Moreover, all too often in our haste to tap the change and development in children we forego opportunities to assess the growth and change in adults.[3]

NOTES

1. Much of the following discussion is taken from J. Teele, "Black Family, Voluntary Association, and Educational Bureaucracy," a paper presented at the 1969 American Sociological Association meetings in San Francisco.

2. See Eugene Litwak and Henry Meyer, "A Balance Theory of Coordination Between Bureaucratic Organizations and Community Primary Groups," Administrative Science Quarterly, June 1966, pp. 31-58.

3. For one of the few books dealing with adult potential for change see Orville Brim and Stanton Wheeler, Socialization After Childhood (New York: John Wiley, 1966).

8

In previous chapters I have chronicled the early development of Operation Exodus and an evaluative research project on the organization's main activity, a private intracity school busing project. The organization from top to bottom was constituted by and run by black "nonprofessional" parents. Problems faced by these parents in their effort to broaden educational opportunities for their children have been partially described, although the main purpose of the book was to describe the problems encountered by the author in his attempt to evaluate the effectiveness of the school busing program. These problems were presented in Chapters 4 and 5, and, in view of their magnitude, it is satisfying that any research took place.

The reader can of course draw his or her own conclusions about the research strategy employed as well as about the findings. Questions may rightly be raised about the concentration of effort on the children in the program, a decision that deflected attention previously focused on the parents who formed Exodus. Or the reader may question the decision—occasioned in part by financial considerations—to assess the effects of the program on children after only a one-year exposure. Alternatively, the reader may concentrate attention on the manner in which research decisions once taken were or were not carried out. Indeed, one of the purposes in writing about Operation Exodus was to focus attention on problems of evaluative research, a much-neglected field.

It is hoped that this book will stimulate thinking about varieties of strategies and tactics in evaluative research among social scientists and educators. It is also hoped, of course, that the book will stimulate serious thought about the nature and function of the educational enterprise in America, particularly as it has been and is being experienced by minorities.

In this chapter I will present a very brief review of the main problems encountered in the research and of the findings, and discuss what appear to me to be some of the implications of this attempt at evaluation of Operation Exodus.

PROBLEMS ENCOUNTERED DURING
RESEARCH IMPLEMENTATION

As indicated in Chapter 3, the effects of the busing program on the children were to be assessed through the use of a quasiexperimental design. The design called for 250 new children in grades 3-6, enrolling in Exodus and being transported to predominantly white schools in Boston for the first time in September 1967, to be compared on change measures with a control group of 250 children never in Exodus and attending predominantly black schools in the black neighborhoods of Boston. It was estimated that all new enrollees would be registered by the middle of August 1967. The investigator had considered this to be a realistic estimate, arrived at after lengthy deliberations.

However, there were fewer than 15 new families registered by the middle of August, which threw the researcher's timetable off. When registration finally did take place in early September, a surprisingly small number of new enrollees were registered; there were only 75 new families and 95 new children, even when grades 7-8 were added in order to increase the sample size. Several factors that might have contributed to the small enrollment were discussed in Chapter 4 and need not be repeated here. I only wish to emphasize that the later problems associated with sample size were a result of the small enrollment in 1967.

A second disappointment almost automatically followed from the late registration of new program enrollees; the control group was also late in being secured and tested. Moreover, for reasons discussed in Chapter 4, only 40 non-Exodus children were obtained for the control group. This disappointment convinced the investigator that a control group study was unlikely to be fruitful, and so a decision was made to change the basic research frame to cohort analysis. It was decided to compare children from the 1966-67 academic year who had spent one year in the program as of September 1967 with children who were just entering the program in September 1967.

The particulars of this patched-up design, similar to Campbell and Stanley's "Recurrent Institutional Cycle Design," have been presented in Chapter 5. Perhaps the main problem confronting the use of this alternative strategy was the program dropout problem, itself further complicated by considerable test attrition. These problems of mortality and test attrition have been fully discussed in Chapter 5, along with steps to be taken to guard against misinterpretation of results obtained from the use of the patched-up design. It was suggested that the patched-up design, combining certain features of both cross-sectional and longitudinal designs, would in the event of substantive cohort differences rule out alternative explanations of testing, regression, mortality, instrumentation, history, and selection. Further, during the data analysis phase, steps were taken that allowed maturation to be ruled out as a competing hypothesis. The reader is referred to Chapters 4-6 for a full discussion of these problems and of the solutions and precautions taken by the investigator.

BRIEF SUMMARY OF FINDINGS ON THE CHILDREN

The cross-sectional study, a comparison of the 1966 cohort of one-year veterans with the 1967 cohort of new Exodus children, reported on in Chapter 6, shows that substantial improvements in reading achievement were registered by Exodus children as a result of spending one year in the program. This finding was supported when similar results were obtained in a longitudinal or "change" analysis and appears to be stable. Self-perception (child's perception of extent of liking by classmates) was also a focus of the study. In the cross-sectional analysis, children in the 1966 cohort showed more positive estimation of being liked by classmates than children in the 1967 cohort. This finding was not supported by longitudinal analysis. Neither Coleman's measure of fate control nor an index of self-image (both consisting of attitude scale items) differentiated between cohorts, nor were these latter two measures related to achievement for either cohort. Problems of test attrition and small sample size, along with the unreliability of attitude items, however, demand that these negative results on attitudes be viewed cautiously.

It was also found that among children who had spent a year in the program at the time of pretesting a relationship existed between the child's feeling of the extent to which his classmates liked him and his reading achievement, with children who felt best or well liked placing higher on reading achievement than their counterparts. No such relationship was found for children in the 1967 cohort who were just entering the program. However a case analysis for some of the children in the 1967 cohort, which considered changes over time, showed that the relationship between feelings of acceptance and reading ability was quite complex. For example, there are cases in which a child's achievement score declined over the year while his estimate of the degree to which his classmates liked him increased; some children showed circumstantial evidence of having neglected their studies while concentrating on getting along with classmates. Other cases involved children who made substantial gains in reading ability but "deteriorated" over the year in the extent to which they perceived themselves as being liked by classmates. On the basis of my own results it seems that social scientists and educators should undertake more research into children's affective development and into the relationship between affect and cognition.

Responses to questions posed to the parents at the end of the 1967-68 school year, focusing on their subjective evaluation of the educational experience of their children, did not show any large differences between parents in the two cohorts. However, when parents were asked to indicate how many white friends their children had at school, parents of children completing their second year in Exodus indicated that their children had white friends to a far greater extent than parents of children completing their first year.

BRIEF SUMMARY OF FINDINGS ON THE PARENTS

Since the investigator considered the development of the parents to be an important evaluative criterion, an effort was made to chronicle the growth of the organization. Some of the organization's achievements were striking, and its impact on specific program development and over-all influence on the black community was profound. In addition, individual profiles of some of the leaders of Operation Exodus were presented. The profiles provide dramatic evidence of the parents' ability to learn and develop skills. These parents tackled and mastered many problems that were new to them, and individually as well as collectively their achievements offer evidence of the program's success.

IMPLICATIONS OF FINDINGS FOR
EDUCATIONAL PROGRAMS

The main substantive finding from this attempt at evaluation of the effects of busing on the children in Exodus is clear. Over-all there was improvement in reading achievement (the most reliable of the effect or output measures employed in the study), although a few of the children showed deterioration in their academic performance. The main implication of this finding, it seems, is that while busing is not necessarily a panacea for the educational problems of all black children, there are certainly some who may derive academic benefits from attendance at integrated schools, especially if such attendance is on a voluntary basis. Busing is just one of the possible alternatives that should be available to those who are anxious to maximize their children's educational opportunities.

The finding of a relationship between the child's perception of the extent to which his classmates liked him and his reading achievement after completion of one year in the program also has an important implication: those planning school integration programs for black children should be at least as concerned with issues and conditions of emotional and social development as they are with issues of cognitive development. Aggregate findings as well as the case studies presented in Chapter 6 suggest a variety of factors that need to be considered by those involved in the planning of school integration programs. These are, as a minimum, the child's personality, including his feelings and aspirations; the school and classroom atmosphere; the community atmosphere; and conditions at home. Conducive rather than destructive conditions and atmospheres should be maximized if children are to learn,[1] though to be sure some children will learn even in hostile or rejecting atmospheres.

There is one implication at least that results from the consideration of the adults in Exodus and the evidence of their collective and individual achievements. This is that more thought should be given to programs—and their evaluation—designed to heighten the parents' and subsequently the children's interest in the educational process.[2] Perhaps the persisting need to adapt to the politics of education over the years has resulted in an as yet unrecognized large reservoir of creative talent among blacks, in Boston and elsewhere. I have endeavored in Chapter 7 to describe this talent in part by discussing some of the organizational and individual accomplishments of Exodus. It was felt that organizational development as well as the career development of adult individuals in minority community organizations is valuable as an adjunct of evaluation. In the field of education especially there is much discussion of the role of the family in the child's school progress but little research into parent development.

In the case of the adults who led Exodus, and they were more than a few, there can be no doubt of the success of the program. The fact that Exodus became the fulcrum of educational concerns in the community, that it broadened awareness in others of school inadequacies, and that it generated other educational options for blacks in the community all support the claim of its effectiveness, since these were from the beginning stated goals of the parents who formed Operation Exodus.

IMPLICATIONS OF THE STUDY FOR EVALUATION RESEARCH

Social science researchers are coming increasingly under examination from a relatively new source—those on whom they would conduct research. We are growing accustomed to government regulations and procedures that admonish us to observe the rights of privacy and confidentiality. These government admonitions are of course monitored by government officials on an irregular basis and usually from distant places. We are also accustomed to overcoming the difficulties of conducting research in private and public agencies that have their own preconditions. We now need to be concerned with the increasing demand for relevant research; not only are community residents demanding relevancy but many of our colleagues are suggesting that we undertake an effort to study significant problems, be it "pure" or evaluative research. What we have come to recognize is that the proliferation of services, of intervention programs, and especially of innovative educational experiments requires evaluative research. While social scientists know a great deal about the standard and general requirements for evaluative research, we know less about the specific problems encountered in evaluation research, especially in sensitive research areas such as education, a gap with which this volume is concerned. Although such sensitive research can be most difficult, it needs to be done. I believe also that sensitive evaluation research can be done.*

I shall briefly discuss here several aspects of evaluation research that have arisen from the present study that are strongly related to the demand for relevancy being voiced increasingly by our target subjects and by study groups.

The first aspect concerns the relation of the researcher to the researched. There is a great need in evaluative research in sensitive areas for the investigator to win the trust of those whom he would study. The investigator must be prepared to spend a good deal of time in the development of this trust, and he must establish the relationship before he undertakes research. Perhaps he can best undertake this research if he is not under the pressure of "publish or perish." The investigator who wishes to support himself and/or a professional staff must guard against a premature evaluative research effort, which is most difficult when important innovations are already under way. However, in the case of an investigator who is "independent" and not under pressure for quick results, patience and the establishment of trust can be rewarding.

---

*The price our society pays for weak evaluative research in this area is a high one, especially the price paid by black parents seeking educational opportunities for their children: witness the unfortunate publicity that too often attends poor research on busing. An example of such research is David Armor's "The Evidence on Busing," The Public Interest, Summer 1972, pp. 90-126. For a comprehensive critique of Armor's paper see Pettigrew et al., op. cit.

In the evaluation of Operation Exodus the investigator was more interested in giving assistance to the program staff as a volunteer consultant than in research activity. As discussed in Chapter 2, the initiative for research came from the parents and not from the investigator. When this initiative by the parents led to a research design and money was unavailable for research assistance, the investigator simply asked for parent volunteers to be trained as interviewers and research assistants. Later, when grants were obtained, the now skilled parent-researchers were properly reimbursed for their efforts, and when the present research project had been completed many of those parents were able to find research jobs elsewhere. The fact that parents participated in the design of early research was one of the unique features of this project. Their participation not only provided them with skills but so enhanced the development of trust that later on they felt able to permit the researcher to undertake wider and more comprehensive research.

It would seem that the implications that grow out of this discussion of the relationship between the researcher and the researched are that a genuine collaboration between the researcher and the researched can be a prelude to effective research and that those interested in evaluation research should more often consider its utility. Certainly the problem of objectivity must be a concern in such research, but with care and patience it should be possible to overcome the pitfalls such collaboration may pose. In the case of Exodus, the more the parents learned about research and its problems and the firmer their trust in the investigator, the more willing they were to permit the study to take place. Indeed, they seemed far more interested in research than the school officials.

The second point I wish to consider that should be of interest to students of evaluation research grows logically out of the foregoing and has to do with community participation in the research process. Actually this is simply broader collaboration with the group to be studied.

It seems that in Boston in recent years a growing number of persons have become intolerant of traditional academic research. In Boston's black community there has been growing agitation over the following concerns: the lack of feedback of research results, apparent failure of researchers to think deeply about the use of research results, and an apparent unconcern of some researchers with the rights of subjects. (While the hard-won academic right of the researcher to conduct his investigation without interference must be preserved, it need not and should not take place at the expense of the subject's rights.) As a result of this increase in community concern over research, representatives of several organizations including Exodus came together under the egis of Boston's Black United Front and in 1970 created an autonomous Community Research Review Committee.[3] The essential function of this committee is to bring into balance the rights of researchers and the rights of individual research subjects.

Students of evaluative research may in the future have to be more concerned about the potential uses of their findings. They may be called upon to justify their research designs to community review committees. Indeed, the development of local research review committees may provide a much-needed stimulus and force evaluation researchers to think their problems through more carefully. Moreover, it may well be that the blocking by politicians and others of research in politically sensitive areas will be impossible when the community's residents organize for research.

CONCLUSION

The evaluation effort that has been presented here was made possible through the initiative of a group of black parents in Boston who were concerned about their children's education. This book was written because it was felt that the problems encountered in the attempt to conduct evaluative research in the politically sensitive area of busing should be published for the benefit of students of evaluative research, educators, school politicians, and parents. These problems have been documented as fully as possible. Research implementation difficulties at both the city and neighborhood levels made this an exceedingly difficult research project, and in fact caused changes of research strategy along the way. Fortunately, since the investigator anticipated some difficulties, the possibility for change of strategy had been built into the evaluative design. As described in Chapters 5 and 6, the strategy involved a switch from a control-group design to cohort analysis.

The need for evaluative research is so great, and the attendant gains in knowledge that result from the documentation of problems met in evaluative research undertakings are so valuable, that social scientists should rise to meet the challenge of action or evaluation research. Social scientists will have to be both rigorous and flexible in the development of research strategy.[4] Furthermore, they must not only guard against the invasion of privacy and protect the rights of subjects; they must also guard against political interference. They may even have to overcome initial community resistance to their research efforts.

Admittedly, the study reported on here allows only limited conclusions to be drawn. I have tried to warn the reader in various places where results have to be cautiously viewed. The reading test score change, however, appears to be real. This study thus takes its place with an increasing number of studies suggesting that black children will respond positively to school busing. Some recent writers have suggested that studies of busing have yielded a mixed bag of findings, and this is true enough; but it may also be true that studies have not been well enough designed and implemented to adequately assess the effects of busing. Moreover, as many writers have indicated, it is important to know something about the process and the quality of busing before judgment is passed.[5]

I wish to emphasize, however, that many blacks rightly question the need to bus their children. Recent studies support their contention that neighborhood schools can be made responsive to their children's educational needs. For example, Robert L. Hamblin and his associates in St. Louis concluded on the basis of their experiments that

> When inner city children are placed in an appropriate learning environment with meaningful reinforcers for learning, with an appropriate curriculum which supplements language training in their home environment, they learn at a rate at least equal to or above the national norms.[6]

Certainly the time has come for psychologists, educators, and social scientists to stop making their living by blaming black children and their parents for all of the grave problems that obstruct the education of black children. Unfortunately much attention has been given recently to concepts or notions that in effect continue the tradition of blaming black children for their learning problems.

One such notion is that of heritability estimates, a statistical manipulation designed to assess the relative degree to which genetic or environmental influences account for the variance in cognitive test scores. Christopher Jencks and his associates are the latest academicians to use this deceptive tool.[7] If Jencks and his associates are correct in stating that the burden of eliminating the inequalities in our society should not be placed on the schools, it is still appropriate to consider educational reforms that could make schools more effective at the task of teaching children, black and white.

One gets the same feeling from reading Jencks as one gets from reading Arthur R. Jensen[8]—that he would like to leave blacks right where he concludes they are, some 15 points behind whites in cognitive test results.* Although he alters the heritability estimates presented

---

*In an excellent analysis of Jensen's article Liam Hudson demonstrates the utter poverty of Jensen's work, showing weaknesses

by Jensen, Jencks and his associates salvage what they can; while Jensen estimated that 80 percent of the variance in IQ scores is explained by genetic factors, Jencks suggests that the correct figure is more like 45 percent.

Jerry Hirsch and others have spelled out the trivial and deceptive nature of the concept of heritability.[9] As Hirsch has indicated, a heritability estimate tells us nothing about how a given individual might have developed under conditions different from those in which he actually did develop. Moreover, heritability estimates are incorrectly interpreted as indicators of educability. Jencks argues that it would be too costly to society to try to bring blacks up to the level of whites in cognitive test results. While I am not at all of the opinion that blacks are everywhere as concerned about cognitive skills as Jencks and his associates define them, I am sure that many, many blacks want their children to learn the skills needed for competing in this society. Academics do blacks an injustice by largely ignoring the burdens that our society placed and places on blacks while brooding about what it would cost to treat blacks fairly.

One of the "costs" that depress academics like Jencks is expressed in the term "forced busing," the second of the two phony notions I wish to inveigh against. In Boston the distant as well as the recent history of black experience with the public educational institution suggests that since 1800 or even earlier, educational policies have been pursued that amount to deprivation of opportunity for black children. Thus blacks have been forced into many battles on behalf of their children's education. I have written about one group of black parents who formed an organization, raised money, collected many white allies, and bused their children voluntarily; yet in a real sense they were forced to bus their children.

Just what does "forced busing" mean? Does it mean that those school committeemen who have used every trick in the book to deprive black children and who have shown extreme reluctance to share educational decision-making with blacks should not be constrained by law or judicial decision to take steps to improve the educational opportunities of blacks? Obviously the term "forced bussing" often reflects a case of waffling on the education of black children. Many millions of children, both black and white, have taken buses to school for years in both the north and the south, and no one worried about their being bused.

---

in sampling and in the IQ tests employed. Moreover, Hudson shows that the twins studies used by Jensen present data that are as open to an environmentalist interpretation as to a genetic one. See The Cult of the Fact (London: Jonathan Cape, 1972).

I am not an all-out advocate of busing, but neither do I think any useful purpose would be served for blacks by denying them the opportunity to bus their children to majority white schools on public funds if they want to. Certainly the experience of the children in Exodus supports the notion that academic improvement was one effect of busing. Rather than inveighing against busing, we should be trying to establish optimal educational techniques and strategies designed to capitalize on the learning ability children have, and we should be aware of the arrogance and ignorance of those who argue that black children cannot learn.

NOTES

1. Thomas F. Pettigrew, Clarence Normand, Elizabeth L. Useem, and Marshall S. Smith "Busing: A Review of 'The Evidence'" The Public Interest, (Winter 1973), pp. 88-118.

2. For one such project, which focused on parent and institution effects, see the report prepared by Kirschner Associates, Inc., for the U.S. Office of Child Development, A National Survey of the Impacts of Head Start Centers on Community Institutions (Albuquerque, N.M., 1970).

3. The author, presently a member of the Community Research Review Committee, is preparing a paper on the Committee's activities. The committee's guidelines are presented in Jay Katz, Experimentation with Human Beings (New York: Russell Sage Foundation, 1972), pp. 1034-1036.

4. For an excellent recently published collection of essays on the development of strategies in evaluation research, see Francis G. Caro, Readings in Evaluation Research, (New York: Russell Sage Foundation, 1971).

5. Pettigrew, et al., op. cit.

6. See Robert L. Hamblin, David Buckholdt, Daniel Ferritor, Martin Kozloff, and Louis Blackwell, The Humanization Process (New York: Wiley-Interscience, 1971), p. 264.

7. Christopher Jencks, et al., Inequality (New York: Basic Books, 1972).

8. Arthur R. Jensen, "How Much Can We Boost IQ and Scholastic Achievement?" Harvard Educational Review, Winter 1969, pp. 1-123.

9. Jerry Hirsch, "Behavior-Genetic Analysis and Its Biosocial Consequences," Seminars in Psychiatry, II, 1 (1970), 2(1), 89-105.

FALL 1967 QUESTIONNAIRE, GRADES 3-4

Mark the space on the sheet which is correct for you for each of the questions below. You may leave any question you do not want to answer.

1. Which one are you? _____Boy _____Girl

2. How old are you now?

   _____7 or younger _____8 _____9 _____10 _____11 or older

3. Are you . . .

   _____Negro _____American Indian _____Puerto Rican
   _____Other

4. What school do you attend this year? _____

5. What school did you go to last year? _____

   a) What school did you go to before you started here? _____

   b) When did you first start attending your present school? ____

6. How many people live in your home? Count mother, father, brothers, sisters, aunts, uncles, grandparents, and any others who live with you. Count yourself but don't count your pets.

   _____2 _____3 _____4 _____5 _____6 _____7 _____8
   _____9 _____10 _____11 or more

7. How many children (under 18) are in your family? _____1 (only me) _____2 _____3 _____4 _____5 _____6 _____7
   _____8 _____9 _____10 or more

8. Do you live with your mother? _____Yes _____No

9. Do you also live with your father? _____Yes _____No

10. Does your mother go to work?

    _____Yes _____No _____I don't have a mother

11. Did anyone read to you before you started going to school?

_____No _____Yes, sometimes _____Yes, a lot _____I don't remember

12. Does anyone in your home speak a language other than English most of the time? (Spanish, Italian, Polish, German, etc.)

_____Yes _____No

13. Do you speak a language other than English outside of school?

_____Yes _____No

14. How many rooms are there in your home? Count only the rooms your family lives in. Count the kitchen (if separate) but not bathrooms.

_____1 _____2 _____3 _____4 _____5 _____6 _____7

_____8 _____9 _____10 or more

15. Does your family have a television set?

_____Yes _____No

16. Does your family have a telephone?

_____Yes _____No

17. Does your family have a record player, hi-fi, or stereo?

_____Yes _____No

18. Does your family have a refrigerator?

_____Yes _____No

19. Does your family have a dictionary?

_____Yes _____No _____I don't know

20. Does your family have an encyclopedia?

_____Yes _____No _____I don't know

21. Does your family have an automobile?

_____Yes _____No

22. Does your family have a vacuum cleaner?

_____Yes _____No

23. Does your family get a newspaper every day?

_____Yes _____No

24. Did you read any books last summer? Don't count magazines, weekly readers, or comic books.

_____No   _____Yes, 1 or 2   _____Yes, about 5

_____Yes, about 10   _____Yes, more than 10

25. On school days, how much time do you watch TV at home?

_____None or almost none   _____About 1/2 hour a day

_____About 1 hour a day   _____About 1 1/2 hours a day

_____About 2 hours a day   _____About 3 hours a day

_____Four or more hours a day

26. How many different schools have you gone to since the first grade?

_____1 (only this school)   _____2   _____3   _____4

_____5 or more

27. If you had your choice, would you rather go to another school than this one?

_____Yes   _____No   _____I'm not sure

28. Do most of your classmates like you?

_____Yes   _____No

29. How good a student are you?

_____One of the best students in my class

_____Above the middle of my class   _____In the middle of my class

_____Below the middle of my class   _____Near the bottom of my class

30. How good a student does you mother want you to be in school?

_____One of the best students in my class

_____Above the middle of the class   _____In the middle of my class

_____Just good enough to get by   _____Don't know or doesn't apply

31. Most of the children in this class are:

_____Very Smart   _____Pretty Smart   _____Not Too Smart

32. Did you have a Negro teacher last year? Don't count substitutes.

_____Yes   _____No

Do you have a Negro teacher this year?   _____Yes   _____No

Have you ever had a Negro teacher?   _____Yes   _____No

If yes, what grade was that? _____

33. How many of your friends are white?

_____None   _____A few   _____About half   _____Most of them
_____All of them

34. Did you go to kindergarten?

_____Yes   _____No

35. Did you go to nursery school before you went to kindergarten?

_____Yes   _____No   _____I don't remember

36. What grade were you in last year?

_____First   _____Second   _____Third

37. How long does it take you to get from your home in the morning to school?

_____10 minutes   _____20 minutes   _____30 minutes
_____45 minutes   _____One hour or more

38. How do you usually come to school in the morning?

_____By automobile   _____Walk or bicycle   _____School bus
_____Bus (other than school bus), train, trolley, or subway
_____Other

Look around your class and then look at each of the pictures above. There are four questions about these pictures. For each question check the blank that has the same letter as the picture you choose.

39. Find the picture that looks most like the children in your class now.

    _____A _____B _____C _____D

40. Find the picture that looks most like the children in your class last year (1966-67).

    _____A _____B _____C _____D

41. Find the picture that looks most like the children in your class the year before last.

    _____A _____B _____C _____D

42. Find the picture that looks most like your good friends.

    _____A _____B _____C _____D

43. (For Third Graders Only:) Did you attend Project Head Start?

    _____Yes _____No, but attended another preschool program
    _____No

130

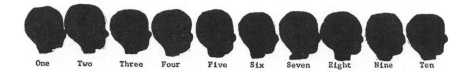

One   Two   Three   Four   Five   Six   Seven   Eight   Nine   Ten

44. Look at the drawing at the top of the page. Make believe that they are pictures of some of the children in your class. The first child, number 1 on the numbers below the picture, is the best liked boy or girl in the class. The least liked is number ten. I want you to decide about where you belong in the line and put a circle around the right number. If you think you are the best liked person in your class, put a circle around number one. If you are near the best liked, you might circle number two or three. If you are near the middle, you might circle four, five or six. The less liked you are, the higher the number you should circle on the row of numbers. If you think you are near the least liked, but not quite, you circle number nine. If you are the least liked of all the children, circle number ten.

45. Do as many of your classmates like you as you want to like you?

_____ Yes (enough)   _____ No (not enough)

46. What things do you like best about this school? Circle the ones you think are true:

(1) The teachers help you a lot.

(2) The teachers seem to like me.

(3) The children seem to like me.

(4) The building is pretty.

(5) I learn a lot.

47. What things do you dislike about this school? Circle the ones you think are true:

(1) The building is ugly.

(2) There's a lot of fighting.

(3) The teachers don't help you enough.

(4) The children are not friendly enough.

(5) The teachers don't seem to like me.

131

48. Would you like to stay here next year or go to a different school?

_____Stay Here   _____Go to a Different School

49. What do you want to be when you grow up?

50. Do you think you'll be able to be what you want to be?

_____Yes   _____No

MY CLASS

We would like to find out how you feel about your class. Here are 20
sentences about a class. I am going to read each sentence to you.
You are to ask yourself, "Does this sentence tell about my class?"
Then mark the answer you like best. Do it like this:

SAMPLE

A. I go to school   (Yes) No I'm not sure

B. We go to school on Saturday   Yes (No) I'm not sure

---

1. It is hard to make real friends in this
   class   Yes No I'm not sure

2. Nearly everyone in this class wants to
   work hard.   Yes No I'm not sure

3. The children in this class are happy
   and pleased when you do something
   for them.   Yes No I'm not sure

4. Many children in this class are not
   fair.   Yes No I'm not sure

5. We need a better classroom to do
   our best work.   Yes No I'm not sure

6. Nearly everyone minds his or her
   own business.   Yes No I'm not sure

7. You can really have a good time in
   this class.   Yes No I'm not sure

8. One or two children in this class
   spoil everything.   Yes No I'm not sure

9. Everyone tries to keep the classroom
   looking nice.   Yes No I'm not sure

10. We don't have a lot of the things we
    need to do our best work.   Yes No I'm not sure

11. The children in this class are pretty
    mean.   Yes No I'm not sure

12. A lot of children in this class don't
    like to do things together.   Yes No I'm not sure

13. Everyone gets a chance to show what
    he or she can do.   Yes No I'm not sure

14. Nearly everyone in this class is polite.   Yes   No   I'm not sure

15. I don't feel as if I belong to this class.   Yes   No   I'm not sure

16. Most of the children in this class do not want to try anything new.   Yes   No   I'm not sure

17. Nearly everyone in this class can do a good job if he or she tries.   Yes   No   I'm not sure

18. A lot of the children look down on others in the class.   Yes   No   I'm not sure

19. You can trust almost everyone in this class.   Yes   No   I'm not sure

20. We do a lot of interesting things in this class.   Yes   No   I'm not sure

MY SCHOOL

Now we would like you to tell us how you feel about your school. Here are some things that some boys and girls say about their school. Are these things true about your school? If they are very true for your school, circle the big "YES!" If they are pretty much true, but not completely true, circle the little "yes." If they are not completely untrue, circle the little "no." If they are not at all true, circle the big "NO!"

1. The teachers in this school want to help you.   YES!   yes   no   NO!

2. The teachers in this school expect you to work too hard.   YES!   yes   no   NO!

3. The teachers in this school are really interested in you.   YES!   yes   no   NO!

4. The teachers in this school know how to explain things clearly.   YES!   yes   no   NO!

5. The teachers in this school are fair and square.   YES!   yes   no   NO!

6. The boys and girls in this school fight too much.   YES!   yes   no   NO!

7. This school has good lunches in the cafeteria.

YES!   yes   no   NO!

8. This school building is a pleasant place.

YES!   yes   no   NO!

9. The principal in this school is friendly.

YES!   yes   no   NO!

10. The work at this school is too hard.

YES!   yes   no   NO!

11. What I am learning will be useful to me.

YES!   yes   no   NO!

12. The trip to and from school is too long.

YES!   yes   no   NO!

13. I wish I didn't have to go to school at all.

YES!   yes   no   NO!

14. This is the best school I know.

YES!   yes   no   NO!

15. The work at this school is too easy.

YES!   yes   no   NO!

16. I work hard in school but don't seem to get anywhere.

YES!   yes   no   NO!

17. I've learned more this year than any earlier year.

YES!   yes   no   NO!

How long do you want to go to school?   (Check one)

_____Only until I'm old enough to quit

_____Through high school but no more

_____I want to go to college

FALL 1967 QUESTIONNAIRE, GRADE 5-8

Mark the space on the answer sheet corresponding to the answer that is correct for you for each question. Mark only one answer for each question. You may leave out any question you prefer not to answer.

1. Are you a boy or girl?

    (A) Boy   (B) Girl

2. How old are you now?

    (A) 9 or younger   (B) 10   (C) 11   (D) 12   (E) 13 or older

3. Where were you born?

    (A) In this city, town, or country   (B) Somewhere else in this state

    (C) In another state in the U.S.   (D) In Puerto Rico   (E) In Mexico

    (F) In Canada   (G) In some other country   (H) I don't know

4. Which one of the following best describes you?

    (A) Negro   (B) White   (C) American Indian   (D) Oriental

    (E) Other

5. Are you Puerto Rican?

    (A) Yes   (B) No

6. Are you Mexican American?

    (A) Yes   (B) No

7. How many people live in your home? Count mother, father, brothers, sisters, aunts, uncles, grandparents, and any others who live with you. Count yourself but <u>don't</u> count your pets.

    (A) 2   (B) 3   (C) 4   (D) 5   (E) 6   (F) 7   (G) 8

    (H) 9   (I) 10   (J) 11 or more

8. How many children (under 18) are in your family? Count yourself.

    (A) 1—only me   (B) 2   (C) 3   (D) 4   (E) 5   (F) 6

    (C) 7   (H) 8   (I) 9   (J) 10 or more

9. Do you live with your father?

   (A)   Yes   (B)   No

10. Do you live with your mother?

   (A)   Yes   (B)   No

11. How far in school did your father go?

   (A)   None, or some grade school   (B)   Completed grade school

   (C)   Some high school, but did not graduate

   (D)   Graduated from high school   (E)   Vocational or business
                                             school after high school

   (F)   Some college, but less than four years

   (G)   Graduated from a four-year college

   (H)   Attended graduate or professional school   (I)   I don't know

12. What kind of work does, or did, your father usually do? If it is
    not in the list below, mark whatever seems to be the closest for
    his main job.

   (A)   Draftsman or medical technician

   (B)   Company executive or government official

   (C)   Store owner or manager, office manager

   (D)   Sales clerk, office or bank clerk, truck driver, waiter, police-
         man, bookkeeper, mailman, barber

   (E)   Salesman

   (F)   Farm owner

   (G)   Farm worker

   (H)   Factory worker, laborer, or gas station attendant

   (I)   Doctor, lawyer, clergyman, engineer, scientist, teacher,
         professor, artist, or accountant

   (J)   Carpenter, electrician, mechanic, tailor, or foreman in a
         factory

   (K)   Don't know

13. Where was your mother born?

   (A)   In this state   (B)   In another state in the U.S.

   (C)   In Puerto Rico

(D) In Mexico   (E) In Canada

(F) In some other country   (G) I don't know

14 How far in school did your mother go?

(A) None, or some grade school   (B) Completed grade school

(C) Some high school, but did not graduate

(D) Graduated from high school

(E) Vocational or business school after high school

(F) Some college, but less than 4 years

(G) Graduated from a four-year college

(H) Attended graduate or professional school   (I) I don't know

15. Does you mother have a job outside your home?

(A) Yes, full-time   (B) Yes, part-time   (C) No

16. Does anyone in your home speak a language other than English most of the time? (German, Italian, Spanish, etc.)

(A) Yes   (B) No

17. Do you speak a language other then English outside of school?

(A) Yes   (B) No

18. Did anyone at home read to you when you were small, before you started school?

(A) No   (B) Once in a while   (C) Many times, but not regularly

(D) Many times and regularly   (E) I don't remember

19. Does your family have a television set?

(A) Yes   (B) No

20. Does your family have a telephone?

(A) Yes   (B) No

21. Does your family have a record player, hi-fi, or stereo?

(A) Yes   (B) No

22. Does your family have a refrigerator?

(A) Yes   (B) No

23. Does your family have a dictionary?

(A) Yes   (B) No   (C) I don't know

24. Does your family have an encyclopedia?

(A) Yes   (B) No   (C) I don't know

25. Does your family have an automobile?

(A) Yes   (B) No

26. Does your family have a vacuum cleaner?

(A) Yes   (B) No

27. Does your family get a newspaper every day?

(A) Yes   (B) No

28. Did you read any books during the last summer? (Do not count magazines or comic books.)

(A) No   (B) Yes, 1 or 2   (C) Yes, about 5   (D) Yes, about 10

(E) Yes, more than 10

29. On school days, how much time do you watch TV at home?

(A) None or almost none   (B) About 1/2 hour a day

(C) About 1 hour a day   (D) About 1-1/2 hours a day

(E) About 2 hours a day   (F) About 3 hours a day

(G) Four or more hours a day

30. How many different schools have you gone to since you started the first grade?

(A) One—only this school   (B) 2   (C) 3   (D) 4   (E) 5 or more

31. Last year how many of the students in your class were white?

(A) None   (B) A few   (C) About half   (D) Most of them

(E) Nearly all of them

32. About how much time do you spend each day on homework? ("Homework" means school assignments that you do at home.)

(A) I have no homework   (B) About 1/2 hour a day

(C) About 1 hour a day   (D) About 1-1/2 hours a day

(E) About 2 or more hours a day

33. If I could change, I would be someone different from myself.

(A) Yes   (B) No   (C) Not sure

34. I can do many things well.

    (A) Yes   (B) No   (C) Not sure

35. I would go to another school rather than this one if I could.

    (A) Yes   (B) No   (C) Not sure

36. I like school.

    (A) Yes   (B) No

37. I sometimes feel I just can't learn.

    (A) Yes   (B) No

38. People like me don't have much of a chance to be successful in life.

    (A) Agree   (B) Not sure   (C) Disagree

39. Most of my classmates like me.

    (A) Yes   (B) Not sure   (C) No

40. How good a student are you?

    (A) One of the best students in my class

    (B) Above the middle of my class   (C) In the middle of my class

    (D) Below the middle of my class   (E) Near the bottom of my class

41. How good a student does your mother want you to be in school?

    (A) One of the best students in my class

    (B) Above the middle of my class   (C) In the middle of my class

    (D) Just good enough to get by   (E) Don't know

42. How good a student does your father want you to be in school?

    (A) One of the best students in my class

    (B) Above the middle of my class   (C) In the middle of my class

    (D) Just good enough to get by   (E) Don't know

43. Did you have a nonwhite teacher last year (for example, Negro, American Indian, Oriental?)

    (A) Yes   (B) No

44. Think now of your close friends. How many of them are white?

    (A) None   (B) A few   (C) About half   (D) Most of them

    (E) All of them

45. Did you go to kindergarten?

(A) Yes (B) No

46. Did you go to nursery school before you went to kindergarten?

(A) Yes (B) No (C) I don't remember

47. What grade were you in last year?

(A) Fourth (B) Fifth (C) Sixth

48. About how long does it take you to get from your home to school in the morning?

(A) 10 minutes or less (B) 20 minutes (C) 30 minutes

(D) 45 minutes (E) One hour or more

49. How do you usually come to school in the morning?

(A) By automobile (E) Walk or bicycle (C) School bus

(D) Train, trolley, subway, or bus other than school bus

(E) Other

50. Is there another public school with your grade as close or closer to your home than this one?

(A) Yes (B) No (C) Don't know

51. Mark the highest grade you want to finish in school.

(A) Grades 6 or 7 (B) Grades 8 or 9 (C) Grades 10 or 11

(D) Grade 12 (E) College

52. Think now who you would like most to have for your classmates. How many of them would be white?

(A) None (B) A few (C) About half (D) Most of them

(E) All of them (F) It doesn't matter

53. When you finish school, what sort of job do you think you will have? Pick the one that is closest.

BOYS ANSWER FROM THE SELECTIONS BELOW	GIRLS ANSWER FROM THE SELECTIONS BELOW
(A) Draftsman or medical technician	(A) Housewife only
(B) Banker, company officer, or government official	(B) Doctor, lawyer, scientist
(C) Store owner or manager, office manager	(C) Beautician

(D) Sales clerk, office clerk, truck driver, waiter, policeman, bookkeeper, mailman, barber

(D) Bookkeeper or secretary

(E) Salesman

(E) Waitress or laundry worker

(F) Farm or ranch manager or owner

(F) School teacher

(G) Farm worker on one or more than one farm

(G) Nurse

(H) Factory worker, laborer, or gas station attendant

(H) Saleslady

(I) Doctor, lawyer, clergyman, engineer, scientist, teacher, professor, artist, accountant

(I) Maid or domestic servant

(J) Carpenter, electrician, mechanic, tailor, or foreman in a factory

(J) Factory worker

(K) Don't know

(K) Don't know

54. How often do you and your parents talk about your school work?

(A) Just about every day   (B) Once or twice a week

(C) Occasionally, but not often   (D) Never or hardly ever

55. Good luck is more important than hard work for success.

(A) Agree   (B) Not sure   (C) Disagree

56. Every time I try to get ahead, something or somebody stops me.

(A) Agree   (B) Not sure   (C) Disagree

57. Since you began school, how many of the students in your classes were white

(A) None   (B) Less than half   (C) About half

(D) More than half   (E) Just about all

58. What was the first grade you attended with students from another race in your class?

(A) First grade   (B) Second grade   (C) Third grade

(D) Fourth grade   (E) Fifth grade   (F) Sixth grade

59. Have you ever had a nonwhite teacher?

(A) Yes   (B) No

If you have had a nonwhite teacher, circle the grade in which you had one. (You may circle more than one.) <u>Don't</u> count substitutes.

(A) First grade   (B) Second grade   (C) Third grade

(D) Fourth grade   (E) Fifth grade   (F) Sixth grade

One   Two   Three   Four   Five   Six   Seven   Eight   Nine   Ten

60. Look at the drawing above. Make believe that they are pictures of some of the children in your class. The first child, number one on the numbers below the picture, is the best liked boy or girl in the class. The least liked one is number ten. I want you to decide about where you belong in the line and put a circle around the right number. If you think you are the best liked person in your class, put a circle around number two or three. If you are near the middle, you might circle four, five, or six. The less liked you are the higher the number you should circle on the row of numbers. If you think you're near the least liked, but not quite, you circle number nine. If you are the least liked of all the children, circle number ten.

61. Do as many classmates like you as you want to like you?

(A) Yes   (B) No

We would like to find out how you feel about your class. Here are 20 sentences about a class. I am going to read each sentence to you. You are to ask yourself, "Does this sentence tell about my class?" Then mark the answer you like best. Do it like this:

SAMPLE

A. I go to school.   (Yes)   No   I'm not sure

B. We go to school on Saturday.   Yes   (No)   I'm not sure

---

1. It is hard to make real friends
   in this class.   Yes   No   I'm not sure

2. Nearly everyone in this class
   wants to work hard.   Yes   No   I'm not sure

3. The children in this class are
   happy and pleased when you do
   something for them.   Yes   No   I'm not sure

4. Many children in this class are
   not fair.   Yes   No   I'm not sure

5. We need a better classroom to
   do our best work.   Yes   No   I'm not sure

6. Nearly everyone minds his or
   her own business.   Yes   No   I'm not sure

7. You can really have a good time
   in this class.   Yes   No   I'm not sure

8. One or two children in this class
   spoil everything.   Yes   No   I'm not sure

9. Everyone tries to keep the class-
   room looking nice.   Yes   No   I'm not sure

10. We don't have a lot of the things
    we need to do our best work.   Yes   No   I'm not sure

11. The children in this class are
    pretty mean.   Yes   No   I'm not sure

12. A lot of children in this class
    don't like to do things together.   Yes   No   I'm not sure

13. Everyone gets a chance to show
    what he or she can do.   Yes   No   I'm not sure

14. Nearly everyone in this class is
    polite.   Yes   No   I'm not sure

15. I don't feel as if I belong in
    this class.   Yes   No   I'm not sure

16. Most of the children in this
    class do not want to try
    anything new.   Yes   No   I'm not sure

17. Nearly everyone in this class
    can do a good job if he or she
    tries.   Yes   No   I'm not sure

18. A lot of the children look down
    on others in the class.   Yes   No   I'm not sure

19. You can trust almost everyone
in this class.   Yes   No   I'm not sure

20. We do a lot of interesting
things in this class.   Yes   No   I'm not sure

MY SCHOOL

Now we would like you to tell us how you feel about your school. Here are some things that some boys and girls say about their school. Are these things true about your school? If they are very true for your school, circle the big "YES!" If they are pretty much true, but not completely true, circle the little "yes." If they are not completely untrue, circle the little "no." If they are not at all true, circle the big "NO!"

1. The teachers in this school
   want to help you.   YES!   yes   no   NO!

2. The teachers in this school
   expect you to work too hard.   YES!   yes   no   NO!

3. The teachers in this school
   are really interested in you. YES!   yes   no   NO!

4. The teachers in this school
   know how to explain things
   clearly.   YES!   yes   no   NO!

5. The teachers in this school are
   fair and square.   YES!   yes   no   NO!

6. The boys and girls in this school
   fight too much.   YES!   yes   no   NO!

7. This school has good lunches in
   the cafeteria.   YES!   yes   no   NO!

8. This school building is a pleasant
   place.   YES!   yes   no   NO!

9. The principal in this school is
   friendly.   YES!   yes   no   NO!

10. The work at this school is too
    hard.   YES!   yes   no   NO!

11. What I am learning will be useful
    to me.   YES!   yes   no   NO!

12. The trip to and from school is too long.	YES!	yes	no	NO!
13. I wish I didn't have to go to school at all.	YES!	yes	no	NO!
14. This is the best school I know.	YES!	yes	no	NO!
15. The work at this school is too easy.	YES!	yes	no	NO!
16. I work hard in school but don't seem to get anywhere.	YES!	yes	no	NO!
17. I've learned more this year than any earlier year.	YES!	yes	no	NO!

How long do you want to go to school? (Check one.)

—— Only until I'm old enough to quit.

—— Through high school but no more.

—— I want to go to college.

INDEX OF NAMES

Neale, Rollin H., 3
Normand, Clarence, 125

Parsons, Theophilus, 3
Pettigrew, Thomas F., 24, 125
Pitts, Barbara, vii
Preston, A., 42
Putnam, George, 4

Roberts, Sarah C., 6
Rogers, David, 55
Rollins, Bryant, 13
Rollins, Judy, 13
Rosen, B., 36
Rosenthal, Robert, 15, 56
Rotter, J., 36
Rubovits, Pamela, 56

Schleifer, Maxwell, 34
Schmidt, William M., vii
Schrag, Peter, 55-56
Seeman, M., 41
Silva, Frank, 12, 112

Sizer, Theodore, viii
Smith, Marshall S., 125
Snyder, John, viii
Srole, L., 36
Stanley, Julian C., 57-60, 65, 69, 116
Stodolsky, Susan, 56
Sumner, Charles, Esq., 5-6

Teele, James, 28, 34, 41, 47, 104, 114
Trotman, Ralph, vii, 13

Useem, Elizabeth L., 125

Weinfield, Frederic, 42
Weinstein, Eugene, 34
Wheeler, Stanton, 114
Wilson, Alan, 31-32
Woodson, Carter G., 17

York, Robert, 42

INDEX OF SUBJECTS

148

ABOUT THE AUTHOR

   JAMES E. TEELE is professor of sociology at Boston University. He received his A.B. degree at Virginia Union University and his Ph.D. degree in sociology at New York University (1961). Dr. Teele was an associate professor at the Harvard School of Public Health before coming to Boston University in 1970. He has authored numerous research papers and monographs in sociology and public health and recently edited Juvenile Delinquency: A Reader (Peacock). He was consultant to the White House Conference on Children in 1970 and is presently consultant to the National Institute of Health.